COOKOUTS
VEGGIE
STYLE!

Jolinda Hackett

Adamsmedia
Avon, Massachusetts

Contains material adapted and abridged from *The Everything® Barbecue Cookbook* by Dale Irwin and Jennifer Jenkins, copyright © 2000 by F+W Media, Inc., ISBN 10: 1-58062-316-6, ISBN 13: 978-1-58062-316-2; *The Everything® Vegetarian Cookbook* by Jay Weinstein, copyright © 2002 by F+W Media, Inc., ISBN 10: 1-58062-640-8, ISBN 13: 978-1-58062-640-8; *The Everything® Vegan Cookbook* by Jolinda Hackett with Lorena Novak Bull, RD, copyright © 2010 by F+W Media, Inc., ISBN 10: 1-4405-0216-1, ISBN 13: 978-1-4405-0216-3; *The Everything® Raw Food Recipe Book* by Mike Snyder with Nancy Faass, MSW, MPH, copyright © 2010 by F+W Media, Inc., ISBN 10: 1-4405-0011-8, ISBN 13: 978-1-4405-0011-4; *The Everything® Being Vegetarian Book* by Alexandra Greeley, copyright © 2009 by F+W Media, Inc., ISBN 10: 1-60550-051-8, ISBN 13: 978-1-60550-051-5.

Published by Adams Media,
a division of F+W Media, Inc.
57 Littlefield Street, Avon, MA 02322. U.S.A.
www.adamsmedia.com

ISBN 10: 1-4405-1240-X
ISBN 13: 978-1-4405-1240-7
eISBN 10: 1-4405-2537-4
eISBN 13: 978-1-4405-2537-7

Printed in the United States of America.

10   9   8   7   6   5   4   3   2   1

Library of Congress Cataloging-in-Publication Data
is available from the publisher.

Readers are urged to take all appropriate precautions before undertaking any how-to task. Always read and follow instructions and safety warnings for all tools and materials, and call in a professional if the task stretches your abilities too far. Although every effort has been made to provide the best possible information in this book, neither the publisher nor the author are responsible for accidents, injuries, or damage incurred as a result of tasks undertaken by readers. This book is not a substitute for professional services.

Many of the designations used by manufacturers and sellers to distinguish their product are claimed as trademarks. Where those designations appear in this book and Adams Media was aware of a trademark claim, the designations have been printed with initial capital letters.

Photos by Sangeeta Kumar

This book is available at quantity discounts for bulk purchases.
For information, please call 1-800-289-0963.

To good times with old friends and the SBC,
and to Tashi, who is my biggest fan.

Acknowledgments

With thanks to Mei for being my unofficial "squished pizza" tester; to the incredibly talented and angelically patient Sangeeta who, like magic, transforms a list of ingredients into amazing photographs; to Teresa Abbate of thefriendlyveg.com, who is indeed a friendly vegetarian; to Lynn and Pete for lovingly grilling up recipes despite winter rains; and finally, to Adrienne, Joey, German, and Ray just for being you.

Contents

Introduction

Many grilling books start off with bombastic imagery describing the primal and communal nature of fire-grilled food, and perhaps a quick history of cooking over the open flame—beginning with ancient man and the cultivation of fire.

To vegetarians, though, all this is of little interest, as it's mostly a history and ethnology of meat.

It wasn't until the late 1990s that vegetarians could walk into just about any grocery store and buy a veggie burger to toss on the grill. Now, vegetarian cuisine has moved past *just* veggie burgers. Unimaginable less than a generation ago, mock meats from chicken tenders to corn dogs fill up grocery aisles and stomachs nationwide.

But the proliferation and evolution of mock meats is only half the story. Our global economy and shrinking planet ships in sauces, spices, and ingredients from every corner of the world. The contemporary vegetarian chef takes good advantage of a rainbow of flavors available right here at home: hoisin sauce from China, curry paste from Thailand, kimchi from Korea, wine from Italy, and cheese from Greece.

This internationally flavored "post-post-meat" era has inspired the new wave of meatless grilling and the variety of global tastes, textures, and ingredients that fill the recipes in this book.

Go out and buy a grill, if you haven't already, and get ready for an onslaught of friends and neighbors oohing, ahhhing, and asking for your recipe secrets. Open up your best bottle of Chardonnay and join me on a journey through the char-grilled flavors of the wonderful fruits, vegetables, cheeses, chocolates, artisan breads, and mock meats that will wake up your taste buds and help you create memorable backyard meals.

Recipes with the leaf symbol are vegan recipes.

Chapter 1

Getting Ready for Your Backyard Feast

If you love your toaster oven almost as much as you love your microwave, stop. Put this book down. It's not for you. Grilling and dining alfresco is pleasurable—it's fun, enjoyable, and a bit of an art form—but it's not for people who just want to thaw out whatever was on sale in the freezer section at the big-box grocery store.

Grilling can be both quick and easy—plugging in your indoor grill or turning the knob on the propane tank to heat up your gas grill is almost as convenient as pressing the buttons on the microwave, but outdoor charcoal grilling takes a bit more work. Much like the rest of the good things in life, what you get out of your grill is only as good as what you put into it. So which option is best for you?

Types of Grills

Grilling is so popular that the market is flooded with options for enthusiasts—both indoor and out.

If you're a bit of a curmudgeon, you don't even need to buy a grill at all! Most beaches, public parks, campsites, and lakesides have public outdoor grills that you can use with your own charcoal. They may require a reservation, or they may be first-come, first-served. These public grills may not be fancy, coverable, or even clean, but your local, state, and federal taxes go toward maintaining them, so why not get your money's worth?

Presuming you would like to own your own grill (for convenience if not for hygiene), you may be a bit confused as to which is best. Welcome to the club. Grilling enthusiasts have been debating the merits of one kind over the others since the discovery of fire. Or at least the invention of gas grills. There are two main adversaries in the Great Grate Debate: charcoal versus gas.

What's the Difference Between Gas and Charcoal Grilling?

On a gas grill, you hook up the unit to a propane tank or natural gas source, and turn it on using the knobs (much like a gas stove). A covered gas grill is ready to go with just a few minutes of preheating.

A charcoal grill is a bit more involved. The charcoal must first be piled and lit, and then the hungry chef must still wait about twenty minutes for the coals to get hot enough to use. The payoff? Food cooked over a real fire and coals rather than gas.

A gas grill may be more convenient, with less mess and quicker preheating, but charcoal purists insist that this is not "real" grilling. Without the genuine flavor of a natural fire, they argue, why even bother?

Charcoal grills get a bit hotter than gas grills, which is important for cooking steak, but not such a big deal when it's tofu and veggies. Smoking with herbs and wood chips is best done on a charcoal grill, but is certainly possible on a gas grill. Other than these small differences, it's mostly a matter of personal preference. And price. With a much simpler setup, charcoal grills are significantly cheaper than gas grills. A basic starter charcoal grill can be as low as $40, whereas gas grills start around $120. If cost is a major factor, however, don't forget the cost of purchasing fuel. In the long run, fueling a gas grill is cheaper than purchasing charcoal.

Consider this: Do you plan on grilling every day? On weeknights? Or are you the occasional backyard party type, who won't be grilling every day but enjoys making it a full experience when you do? For everyday meals, a gas grill is much more convenient, but if grilling is more of a hobby for you than an essential part of dinner, then a charcoal grill will likely give you more satisfaction.

Apartment and townhouse communities may have restrictions on the size and storage of outdoor grills. Charcoal kettle grills may be as small as a bowling ball and will fit comfortably on even the smallest apartment balcony.

Indoor Electric Grills

A third option, an indoor electric grill, is meant to make cooking easy. Infomercials in the '90s bragged about how their fat-cutting grills were suitable for bachelor pads, college dorms, and those with two left feet. The commercials didn't lie: using an indoor grill is as simple as plugging it in.

Indoor grilling may not give you the same elemental, primal satisfaction as cooking over hot coals, but it can be a quick and healthy way to prepare vegetarian meals. Grilling tofu indoors, for example, is much quicker than baking it in the oven, and a lower-fat option compared to frying.

An indoor electric grill can be plugged in outside wherever there's an electrical source. This is particularly convenient on hot days—no need to turn on the oven and heat up the house. With the exception of the smoked recipes, just about every recipe in this book will work on an indoor grill, but some grills may be too small to make things like pizza and full loaves of garlic bread.

Another indoor grilling option is a standup grate that can be placed directly over a gas stove to turn a gas range-top burner into a direct-heat grill. And there's always grill-and-searing pans that can be used on the stovetop; panini presses; and, of course, the famous George Foreman grill and the numerous knockoffs it inspired.

Outdoor grills are sold in home stores or the outdoor section of department stores, whereas indoor grills are stocked in the kitchen and small appliance section. So if you're deciding which to get, be prepared to walk all over the store to make comparisons.

Grilling Accessories

Once you've got your grill and your heat source, whether gas, charcoal, or electric, all you really need to get started are some **long-handled tongs** and a **basting brush,** along with a few basic kitchen tools.

- **Bamboo skewers** are a cheap grilling essential. If you prefer to use reusable metal skewers, look for flat rather than round edges, which hold food in place more securely. Bamboo skewers need to be soaked before using. Fully submerge your skewers in liquid and let them soak for at least 20 minutes, and up to 4 hours. Any longer and they tend to get a bit soft. Sneak a bit of extra flavor into your kebabs by soaking bamboo skewers in wine, juice, or even a bit of rum instead of plain water. Another quick bamboo skewer tip: Soak them all—yes, the whole store-bought bunch—then drain and place in a plastic bag in the freezer. They'll always be ready to go when you need them. As long as they aren't too charred, bamboo skewers can be reused.
- A **grill basket** is convenient for grilling smaller vegetables, such as snow peas, and for shaking up french fries. Choose a grill basket that was designed for vegetables rather than fish. Another option for grilling smaller items is a grill liner or a specially designed barbecue sheet that lies on top of the grates.

- A **long-handled metal spatula** is more convenient than tongs for lifting flat things—think tofu slabs and veggie burgers – off the grill, while keeping grill marks intact. They're an essential for pizza, flatbreads, and delicate stickier foods, like polenta slices.
- **Heavy-duty aluminum foil** is wonderfully convenient—and not just for foil-wrapped "hobo packets." Foil can be folded into makeshift oven mitts, used as a scrub brush for grate cleaning, shaped into a bowl in a pinch, used as a smoker with some wood chips, and used to insulate food if your grill cooks unevenly. On a charcoal grill, foil can help the lazy griller with cleanup. Before you start grilling, line the bottom of the grill completely with foil. Then place the coals on top of the foil. When the party's over (and the coals have cooled), just pick up the foil and toss—no brushing or sweeping needed.
- Keep a **spray bottle filled with water** handy for any little flare-ups. With less fat and grease, vegetarian grilling is much less susceptible to these pesky little flames, but it's still a good idea to keep a spray bottle nearby.

Grill Preparation and Maintenance

Now that you've devoted half a paycheck or so to a shiny new grill, keeping it clean is of utmost importance. Besides being hygienic, cleaning helps the grates last longer, ensures even heat distribution, and makes your food taste better (no burned, charred taste).

For a gas grill, clogged or greasy burners and vents mean uneven heat. Plan on giving your grill a good deep clean once or twice a year, burners and all. If you have a charcoal grill, take it apart and give each individual part a solid soapy scrub.

If you only use your grill seasonally, then the end of the season is the best time for a deep clean. To clean grill grates, you can use a store-bought oven cleaner, but some soap and good old-fashioned elbow grease work just as well. Minimalists prefer just burning off any extra sludge. To do this, fire up a naked grill super hot for about 10 minutes, then carefully scrape off any bits with a wire brush. Heat it up again for another 5 to 10 minutes. Grill grates come in a variety of different materials, so of course it doesn't hurt to check out the owner's manual to see if the manufacturer suggests any specific cleaning techniques.

Give the outside of your grill a good wipe down every so often, too. Normal dish-washing detergent and a gentle sponge will do. Don't forget the inside of the lid.

Every time you fire up the grill, give it a good scrape clean with a wire brush. Don't have a wire brush? Use the old foil technique: crumple up a ball of foil and grasp it with a pair of grill tongs. Use the foil to scrape the hot grill grates.

Some grill experts insist it's best to *not* scrape the grill clean after grilling. Those little bits and blobs of blackened food stuck to the grates are insurance against rusty grates, they say. Leave them there, and save your grill scraping for the next time you fire it up. If you do decide to scrape those bits off, finish the cleaning process with a light oil rubdown to protect against rust. Leftover ash does need to be emptied after each use—once completely cooled, of course.

Ready, Set, Grill!

Grilling can be intimidating for novices, but the good news is that vegetarian grilling is simpler (and safer!) than cooking meat on the grill. A few extra tips and techniques will have you grilling like a pro.

Grill temperatures vary widely, and can even vary from one end of your skewer to the other, so keep a close watch on everything on the grill. When skewering foods, chop vegetables to a uniform size to ensure even cooking, and consider how long each individual ingredient will take to cook, combining ingredients according to cook time. Quicker-cooking veggies, such as soft zucchini, shouldn't be paired on a skewer with firmer foods that take longer, such as carrots. Or cut quicker-cooking foods into larger dices while thinly slicing slower-cooking foods. Of course, even a bit over- or undercooked, most veggies taste great when grilled!

Grill times listed in recipes are always approximate, so use your best judgment. The art of the grill is a delicate dance between patiently *not* checking and moving food around, and avoiding overly charred or burned foods.

Using Direct and Indirect Heat

The most common grilling technique is to place food on the grates directly over the heat source or hot coals (direct heat). Indirect heat (food away from the heat source) is used less frequently in vegetarian grilling than in grilling meat, where it's needed to cook large and thick chunks of meat. Indirect heat can be used for warming pitas and other breads, melting cheese and chocolate, and smoking tofu, but a gentle low heat will work just as well for most vegetarian purposes. One exception is pizza, which needs indirect heat so as not to burn.

On a gas grill, turn on only half of the burners to create two heat zones. The direct heat zone is right over the lit burners, while off to the side, over the unlit burners, is the indirect heat zone. A similar effect can be created using charcoal. Just shove all the charcoal to one side, or, if your grill is large enough, divide the briquettes in half to create two hot zones on either end, leaving the center for indirect heat. On a circular kettle grill, create a ring of charcoal around the edges, leaving an empty space in the center for indirect heating.

On an indoor grill, check your manufacturer's instructions for where the direct and indirect heat areas are. With a small indoor appliance, you may not be able to create two zones at once, but the heat temperature itself should be easily adjustable.

On a gas grill, adjust the heat using the temperature knob. On a charcoal grill, the amount of charcoal and the length of time the briquettes have been burning determine how hot the grill is. Most charcoal takes about 25 minutes to become ready for cooking. After another 30 minutes or so, the charcoal will start to cool, leaving you with medium and then low heat. You can also create low and high heat zones at the same time. Push about ¾ of the charcoal to one side of the grill, leaving ¼ to heat the other side. Fewer briquettes mean less heat. Larger grills may be built with adjustable grates that can be raised or lowered to quickly adjust the cooking temperature.

Flavor Matters

Barbecue is all about flavor. Think of a grilled meal as having three main ingredients: Fire, smoke, and the food itself, including whatever sauces and spices you add. To have the best barbecue on the block, you need the best fire, the best smoke, and, of course, the best foods.

1. Fire is the silent *je ne sais quoi* of grilling, the reason you bought a grill, and the reason you bought this book. There's something about fire that universally draws us in. We all seem to love sitting around a campfire and poking it with a stick, don't we? Hovering around and turning over the barbecue coals is *fun*!

   For a premium fire and premium flavor, charcoal is better. While hardwood charcoal can create a great fire, because it takes longer to ash over and burns quicker (and hotter!) once it does, some backyard cooks find it inconvenient to use. Try a combination of half hardwood and half briquettes for a longer burn time. Use briquettes if you need the fire to last a long time, such as when you're smoking tofu or grilling for a large crowd.

2. The tantalizing aroma of smoke lures us in just as inexplicably as fire does. So great is the love of smoke that food scientists have figured out how to capture it in a bottle and sell it as a flavor additive.

Hardwood charcoal gives off a more rustic, smoky flavor than pressed briquettes, which can impart a less natural, chemical flavor to food.

Add a fresh-scented herbal smoke to your fire by using sprigs of fresh herbs. Soak a bundle of herbs in water for just a few minutes, then place them on the grate off to the side a bit, away from the hottest part of the grill so they don't burn too quickly. Close the lid to keep the smoke contained around the food, or leave it open to enjoy the scent. A few sprigs of fresh rosemary, thyme, or sage will work their aromatherapy magic by whetting appetites and teasing nostrils with a taste of the flavors to come. The smoky flavor is subtle, and takes time to develop, but even if you can't taste the delicate herb flavors, the aroma is lovely and your guests will be impressed with your culinary adventurousness.

For another subtle layer of flavor and five-star presentation, use fresh herbs as kebab skewers. Rosemary and lemongrass work best for this, but firmer stalks of oregano, sage, and lavender can also be used. Remove the leaves (leaving a few on the end for garnish) and soak the stems in water for twenty minutes. Use a bamboo or metal skewer to poke starter holes, then skewer your ingredients on the herb stalks and grill.

To add a stronger smoky flavor, stockpile a variety of wood chips and learn how to use them. They're needed to smoke tofu or seitan, and make a pleasant addition to just about any savory or hearty entrée, such as tempeh and veggie burgers. Each type of wood imparts a subtly different flavor. Hickory, mesquite, and cherry are the most common, but shop around to find just about any hardwood you can imagine. Wine and spirit enthusiasts can even find wood chips made out of old wine- and whiskey-aging barrels.

3. The third ingredient in a grilled meal is the food itself. Use fresh organic produce and always take the time to press your tofu. Freezing tofu first can give it

a chewier, denser texture, which some people prefer. Frozen (then thawed!) tofu will absorb even more of a flavorful marinade. Seitan doesn't need to be pressed, but give it a gentle squeeze to get rid of any extra water hiding inside.

Don't skimp on marinating times, particularly when it comes to tofu, tempeh, and seitan. Unless a recipe indicates otherwise, most marinades can even be prepared the day before your big day and ingredients marinated overnight. Most of the flavor in grilling comes from basting sauces and marinades (along with the smoke and fire), and the barbecue sauces that work on meat work just as well on vegetarian items. Avoid overly sweet sauces with cheap fillers. If the ingredients list includes high fructose corn syrup—don't even *think* about buying it!

What to Grill?

Store-bought veggie burgers work well on the grill. Vegetarian chicken cutlets are a nice change from veggie burgers. Try Gardein or Quorn brands, and keep an eye out for grillable vegetarian "ribs," "beef tips," and even drumsticks. Read the label to check for any specific grilling instructions.

If your patties are a bit soft and tend to fall apart or through the grates, place them on a layer of foil. Veggie burgers cook much more quickly than beef burgers, so keep a close eye on them.

While most mock meats can be grilled, vegetarian hot dogs are hit and miss. Some work well on the grill, and others sort of disintegrate. When shopping for veggie dogs, read the label on the package carefully before you buy them, as some clearly state "Do not grill."

Vegetarian sausages are a different story. Boca and Tofurky brands both make tasty sausages that hold up on the grill. Brush them with a bit of oil, grill, and chow down. Vegetarian sausages need just enough time to get heated through—just a minute or two on each side.

Besides mock meats, most fruits and vegetables can be tossed on the grill. Toss vegetables with just a light brushing of olive oil and a shake of salt and pepper, and give fruit a brush of butter and a drizzle of honey. Oil overpowers the delicate flavor of fruit.

Fruits that you would never dream of cooking transform into a summery treat when grilled. Try bananas, apricots, peaches, nectarines, plums, mangoes, kiwis, papayas, and, of course, pineapple. Keep fruits moist on the grill by soaking them in a bit of water with a squeeze of lemon juice for 20 minutes first.

As for vegetables, corn on the cob, portobello mushrooms, eggplant, and zucchini are a few barbecue favorites, but almost anything you can imagine can be heated on the grill, including broccoli, cauliflower, tomatoes, artichokes, bok choy, romaine lettuce, and cabbage. Even okra!

Root vegetables with less water content are tasty but tend to dry out on the grill. Keep carrots, turnips, parsnips, beets, and sunchokes over lower heat for longer than other vegetables, about 15 to 20 minutes. Serve them with butter or margarine if they're too dry for your taste.

Sharing the Grill

Grilling brings people together for not just a meal, but a party! That means, at least now and then, you'll probably be cooking for vegetarians and omnivores at the same time.

If you're not a vegetarian yourself, you should know and respect that many vegetarians take their dietary preferences quite seriously. If you wouldn't think it harmless to include "just a little bit" of bacon in a meal meant for a kosher Jew, don't do it to a vegetarian, either. Most vegetarians would rather not eat a veggie burger that

has been sitting in the grilling juices left behind by a floppy steak, while others may not be bothered by it. But unless you know your guests' attitudes for certain, better to assume that the vegetarians would prefer the vegetarian foods to be grilled separately from the meats.

Communicate with your vegetarian guests in advance to find out their dietary needs. Do they eat dairy? Eggs? What can you, as a host, do to make them feel comfortable, welcomed, and well fed at your event? If your grill is large enough, divide the grill and cook the vegetarian items well away from the meats, providing a clear delineation between the two areas. Even if you're just warming up buns for the veggie burgers, do it on the vegetarian side. Most vegetarians will be happy with this arrangement.

If your grill is too small to allocate an entire portion for the meatless foods, grill all of the vegetarian foods first. A little leftover tofu char won't bother steak-lovers in the same way that a little steak char may be a deal-breaker for your vegetarian friends.

Just as importantly, as a vegetarian guest, respect a few rules of etiquette and help out your host a bit in advance. If you prefer that your foods not share even a well-cleaned grill with meat items, ask your host if it would okay to bring along a barbecue sheet cover. These sheets are designed to hold smaller items (like diced vegetables) on the grill but have holes which let the good grilled flavor come through while still separating foods from the grate. So vegetarians get a genuinely flame-kissed meal (no foil blocking the good flavor) and everybody is happy. Problem solved. Another option (though less ideal, as far as flavor goes) is to place a layer of heavy-duty aluminum foil over the grill when heating the vegetarian foods. Of course, separating the food from the flame is cheating the vegetarians out of the best part of grilling, but if there's no other option, it's much better than warming up veggie dogs in the microwave. You might suggest this to your host, and bring along an extra roll of foil in case it's needed.

While it may not be the most environmentally friendly option, you can use a disposable grill for the veggie items. These are single-use stand-alone pans that come filled with charcoal and ready to grill. All they need is a light. They cost just a few dollars, and can be used to keep vegetarian items completely separate from the meat. Incidentally, these are also wonderfully convenient for camping trips and tailgating parties.

Whether you're downing pork or portobellos, all cookout attendees can agree that grilling is great fun, especially when accompanied by great company, great weather, and a great beer. After all, that's why you're getting together in the first place.

Chapter 2

Appetizers and Starters

Crisped Camembert and Mango Quesadillas

Serves 6 as an appetizer or 2 as an entrée

4 flour tortillas

Olive oil for brushing

8 ounces Camembert cheese, sliced thin

1 mango, sliced into thin strips

¾ teaspoon chili powder (optional)

¼ cup red or yellow onion, diced

Warmed mango softens and creams together with melting Camembert, creating a silky smooth texture that delicately contrasts with the crispy grilled tortillas in these quesadillas. Camembert works well with the mango, but a French Brie would also work.

1. Lightly brush two flour tortillas with oil on one side and place on work surface, oil-side down.

2. Arrange a thin layer of Camembert cheese on two quesadillas, leaving about ¼" space from the edge. Place mango slices on top of the cheese, and sprinkle with chili powder and onion. Cover each tortilla with another tortilla, to make a "sandwich."

3. Grill over low heat until tortillas are lightly crisped and cheese has softened, about 3–4 minutes, turning once. Slice each quesadilla into six wedges.

Roasted Insalata Caprese

Serves 4

16 cherry tomatoes

12 ounces fresh mozzarella, chopped into 1" cubes, or 12 1-ounce mozzarella balls

12 large fresh basil leaves

1 tablespoon balsamic vinegar

Salt and pepper to taste

A traditional Italian caprese salad is skewered and grilled for an elegant appetizer. Sliver a few extra fresh basil leaves to sprinkle on top.

1. Thread cherry tomatoes, mozzarella, and basil leaves on skewers, alternating ingredients, and place on a well-greased grill.

2. Grill over high heat for just 1–2 minutes on each side.

3. Just before serving, drizzle the skewers with balsamic vinegar and add a dash of salt and pepper to taste.

Halloumi Skewers with Lemon Parsley Chimichurri

Serves 4

1 cup parsley, chopped

1 tablespoon minced shallots

¼ cup olive oil, plus additional for brushing

1 tablespoon red wine vinegar

1 tablespoon lemon juice

1 tablespoon dried oregano

¼ teaspoon red pepper flakes

1 6-ounce package halloumi cheese, sliced ½" thick

Chimichurri, a fragrant green sauce, is a popular marinade for meat in Argentina. Here, it's paired with Greek halloumi cheese in a fusion of South American and Mediterranean cuisines. Prepare the chimichurri sauce in advance, if possible, to allow time for the flavors to come alive.

1. In a blender or food processor, process parsley, shallots, ¼ cup olive oil, red wine vinegar, lemon juice, oregano, and red pepper flakes until almost smooth. Sauce should still be a bit textured.

2. Lightly brush halloumi with olive oil, then thread on skewers. Grill over medium-high heat for about 3 minutes on each side, until softened and well browned. Top with sauce.

What Is Halloumi?

Usually a sheep's milk cheese (though sometimes a blend of sheep and goat milk), halloumi is a cheese native to the Cyprus region of Greece. If you can't find it in your local natural or gourmet foods shop, try a Mediterranean deli.

Charred Edamame

Serves 6 as an appetizer or 3 as a side dish

1 12-ounce package frozen edamame, thawed

2 tablespoons olive oil

Sea salt or kosher salt to taste

You'll need a grill basket or a grill pan in order to cook edamame on the grill. Wrapping the pods in aluminum foil will also work, but won't give you the same smoky outdoor taste.

1. Toss edamame with olive oil. If using fresh edamame, boil in water for 5–6 minutes first. Grill in grill basket, tossing occasionally.

2. Season well with salt.

What's the Difference Between Kosher, Sea, and Table Salt?

The well-trained chef's salt of choice is seldom the powdered table salt most home cooks are familiar with. Instead, they use either crystal sea salt or coarse, flaky kosher salt, both of which are available in most supermarkets. The advantage of the large crystal flakes characteristic of these salts is ease of control. The degree of seasoning is a matter of taste—up to the cook's palate—but kosher salt has less "saltiness" by volume than ordinary table salt. That means a pinch of kosher salt is milder than an equal pinch of table salt, giving the cook a chance to taste and season gradually. The trace minerals in sea salt add a richer depth of flavor than regular table salt. Get rid of your table salt in favor of one of these tastier choices.

Cheddar Jalapeño Poppers

Makes 12 poppers

12 jalapeño peppers

4 ounces cream cheese, softened

¼ cup grated Cheddar, Monterey jack, or Mexican-blend cheese

1 teaspoon lime juice

2 tablespoons green onion, finely minced

4 cloves garlic, minced

Make a lining out of foil to hold these pepper poppers on the grill, or line them up on skewers to keep them in place. For a less fiery popper, remove the seeds from the peppers before stuffing. Can't get enough heat? Add a few splashes of hot sauce to the cream cheese mixture.

1. Slice the top off of each pepper and slit lengthwise. (You may want to wear gloves for this step.)

2. Combine cream cheese, grated cheese, lime juice, onion, and garlic.

3. Stuff cheese mixture into peppers, using a butter knife or a small spoon.

4. Grill over medium heat for 15–20 minutes. If that isn't decadent enough, serve them with ranch dressing for dipping.

Balsamic Bruschetta with Roasted Tomatoes

Makes 12 slices bruschetta

4 medium tomatoes

12 1"-thick slices French baguette or any artisanal bread

Olive oil for brushing, plus an additional ½ teaspoon

1 whole clove garlic, cut in half, plus 2 cloves garlic, minced

¼ cup chopped fresh basil

2 teaspoons balsamic vinegar

¼ teaspoon sea salt

⅛ teaspoon black pepper

¼ teaspoon red pepper flakes (optional)

Look for an artisan Italian bread to kick this recipe up a notch on the gourmet scale. Otherwise, ciabatta or an ordinary French baguette works just fine. If you want to show off your fabulous and expensive Italian olive oil, omit it from the tomato mix and drizzle the finished bruschetta pieces with olive oil in front of your guests— label side out, of course.

1. Slice each tomato in half. Place on a greased grill, cut-side down, and heat for 2–3 minutes, until slightly softened.

2. Brush bread slices with olive oil, grill for 2–3 minutes, until just lightly toasted, then rub with cut garlic clove.

3. Prepare the topping by dicing the grilled tomatoes and tossing with minced garlic, chopped basil, and balsamic vinegar. Add salt, pepper, and optional red pepper flakes.

4. Pile tomato mixture onto each slice of bread.

Beyond Basic Bruschetta

This bruschetta recipe sticks to the basics, combining fresh summer tomatoes with balsamic vinegar, garlic, fresh basil, and toasted bread. But don't let that stop you from experimenting with other ingredients. Try adding diced artichoke hearts, roasted red peppers, avocados, eggplant, or just about any fresh herbs. Whatever you do, don't even *think* about using dried basil instead of fresh when making bruschetta.

Grilled Artichokes with Paprika Aioli

Serves 6

Water for pre-cooking

4 small artichokes, trimmed and chopped in half

1 tablespoon plus ½ teaspoon lemon juice, divided

1 tablespoon olive oil

⅓ cup mayonnaise

2 cloves garlic, minced

1 teaspoon Dijon mustard

½ teaspoon paprika

¼ teaspoon salt or to taste

¼ teaspoon cayenne pepper

A simple mayonnaise-based aioli spiked with paprika and cayenne complements the softened artichokes for a real melt-in-your-mouth effect. Sublime.

1. Boil or steam artichokes for 10–12 minutes, until soft, being sure not to overcook. Allow to cool and dry.

2. Whisk together 1 tablespoon lemon juice and olive oil, and coat artichokes well.

3. Place artichokes cut-side down on the grill, and grill for about 5 minutes, or until lightly charred.

4. Combine remaining ingredients and use as a dip for artichokes.

Grilled Apricot Insalata Caprese

Serves 8

2 teaspoons sugar

3 tablespoons butter or margarine, melted

8 apricots, sliced in half, pit removed

½ pound fresh mozzarella, sliced into ¼"-thick rounds

14–16 fresh basil leaves

2 teaspoons balsamic vinegar

2 teaspoons olive oil

Salt and pepper to taste

This colorful salad spread can be artfully arranged on a serving platter. Alternatively, stack mozzarella slices and basil leaves on top of the grilled apricots to create individual portions.

1. Whisk together sugar and melted butter, and baste apricots. Grill, cut-side down, for 1–2 minutes.

2. Combine apricots, mozzarella, and basil on a serving platter, alternating ingredients to arrange decoratively.

3. Drizzle with balsamic vinegar and olive oil, and sprinkle lightly with salt and pepper.

Balsamic-Brushed Crostini with Avocado Pesto

Makes 12 slices

2 tablespoons olive oil

1 tablespoon balsamic vinegar

12 ½"-thick slices French baguette

⅓ cup pesto

½ large avocado, diced small

Use a homemade vegan pesto to keep these little appetizers suitable for vegans. For variety, instead of topping off the crostini toasts individually, place the avocado pesto in a serving dish and arrange the toasts around the rim. For a variation, add a couple of spoonfuls of chopped marinated artichoke hearts instead of avocado.

1. Whisk together olive oil and balsamic vinegar and brush both sides of bread slices well with the mixture.

2. Grill bread slices for 3–4 minutes each side.

3. Combine the pesto and avocado, being careful not to mash the avocado too much. Spread a small amount on each slice of toasted bread.

Spice-Crusted Halloumi Bites

Serves 8

1 9-ounce package halloumi cheese, sliced ½" thick
Olive oil
3 tablespoons paprika
3 tablespoons garlic powder
1 teaspoon red pepper flakes
1 tablespoon chili powder
½ teaspoon oregano
½ teaspoon cumin
1 teaspoon salt
½ teaspoon fresh ground black pepper

A generous amount of herbs and spices creates a crusty coating on salty grilled cheese. For an appetizer or antipasto platter, slice the halloumi into bite-sized pieces and stick on a toothpick after grilling and cooling slightly.

1. Lightly brush halloumi with olive oil.

2. In a small bowl, combine remaining ingredients. Coat halloumi well with spices, pressing, if needed, to get them to stick.

3. Thread on skewers and place on a well-greased grill for 3–4 minutes on each side, until cheese is lightly crisped on the outside.

Can't Find Halloumi?

Halloumi may be the original, but there are plenty of copy-cat substitutes out there. Canadian cheese makers, hoping to get a slice of the halloumi market, introduced a cheese called Guernsey Girl that, they boast, grills up just like halloumi. Not to be outdone, the United States has also joined the game, with Idaho farmers coming up with a halloumi-style cow's milk cheese called Golden Greek Grillin' Cheese. Yanni brand uses California cows to produce a similar product just called Grilling Cheese. For savory recipes, such as this one, Indian paneer would also substitute well. Just reduce the heat a bit, as paneer chars easily.

Avocado Goat Cheese Quesadillas

Serves 6 as an appetizer or 2 as an entrée

4 flour tortillas

Oil or softened butter for brushing

8 ounces goat cheese

1 avocado, thinly sliced

1 teaspoon lime juice

2 tablespoons chopped fresh cilantro

They're quite filling, but spoiling your appetite has never been so worth it. Serve with sour cream, salsa, or guacamole for dipping. To turn up the heat, add a light sprinkle of minced jalapeño or poblano peppers before grilling.

1. Lightly brush one side of each flour tortilla with softened butter or oil.

2. On unbuttered side, spread half of goat cheese and half of avocado slices on two of the tortillas. Drizzle with lime juice, sprinkle with cilantro, then top each tortilla with another, butter-side up.

3. Grill over medium-low heat for 2–3 minutes on each side. Allow to cool slightly before slicing.

Aussie Onion Blossoms

Serves 3

1 large sweet onion
2 cloves garlic, minced
1 tablespoon cold margarine or butter, cut small
1 tablespoon barbecue sauce

This onion blossom recipe comes with apologies to Australians everywhere, because there's nothing Australian about it—onion blossoms are a purely American invention. To make it even more American, add a generous amount of regional spices in place of the barbecue sauce. Try Old Bay seasoning, a Cajun spice blend, or some good old-fashioned American chili powder.

1. Remove thin papery outer layer of onion and carefully slice onion from top to ¼" above the bottom, to create wedges that are connected at the base. Make 3 cuts to create 6 wedges.

2. Stuff with minced garlic, dot with butter or margarine, and drizzle with barbecue sauce.

3. Spray a sheet of aluminum foil with cooking spray or lightly brush with olive oil to prevent sticking. Wrap onion in foil and grill for 40–45 minutes.

Blackened Baba Ghanoush

Serves 6

2 medium eggplants, pricked with a fork

3 cloves garlic

2 tablespoons lemon juice

2 tablespoons tahini

Salt and pepper to taste

2 teaspoons good quality olive oil (optional)

Pita wedges, for serving

It's cheating, really, to prepare baba ghanoush using any method other than a grill, as the smoky flavor is a key ingredient in traditional preparations. Smashing the eggplant by hand ensures that it keeps a thick and chunky texture, so the charred flavor doesn't disappear. Leftovers make an excellent sandwich spread for vegetarian wrapped sandwiches.

1. Place eggplants directly on the grill and allow to cook until well blackened, about 20–25 minutes.
2. In a small bowl, mix together garlic, lemon juice, and tahini.
3. Slice eggplants in half, scoop out the pulp, and mash together with garlic–lemon juice mixture. Season with salt and pepper to taste, and drizzle with a touch of olive oil just before serving with pita wedges.

Indian Mashed Eggplant

Middle Eastern baba ghanoush is similar to a vegetarian Indian dish called baigan barta. To try it out, add a few Indian spices—1 teaspoon of cumin, 1 teaspoon of garam masala, and a touch of cayenne pepper—and substitute ⅓ cup yogurt for the tahini. Serve it with naan instead of pita bread for an appetizer, or pair it with rice for an entrée. Either way, garnish your eggplant purée with a bit of fresh minced cilantro or parsley—just a touch for color, not too much!

Roasted Garlic

Yields 2 bulbs

2 full heads garlic, unpeeled
2 tablespoons olive oil
2 tablespoons water

Roasted garlic is an invaluable flavoring that can be used in many dishes or served on its own as a spread. Just don't let it burn.

1. Cut ¼" off the very top part of the garlic heads cross-wise and discard. Place garlic heads on a large sheet of heavy-duty aluminum foil. Drizzle with olive oil and water.

2. Close the aluminum foil to make a packet, leaving a little "chimney" for the steam to escape.

3. Heat grill to low heat. Roast garlic for 20 minutes. When cool, you can squeeze garlic cloves out, as you need them for recipes. Store in plastic bags in the refrigerator for future use.

Mushroom Bruschetta

Serves 4

8 1"-thick French baguette or crusty country bread, sliced on a diagonal

4 teaspoons aioli or mayonnaise mixed with chopped garlic

8 ounces white mushrooms, plus ¼ pound mixed specialty mushrooms such as oyster, shiitake, enoki, or portobello (optional)

2 tablespoons olive oil

1 teaspoon mixed dried herbs, such as thyme, oregano, rosemary, and basil

Juice from ½ a lemon

Salt and fresh ground pepper to taste

Fresh chopped parsley or chives (optional)

If you're not entertaining vegans, a curl or two of shaved Parmesan cheese would look nice as a garnish on top of these little toasts.

1. Spread the aioli onto both sides of each slice of bread. Grill until well marked on both sides. Transfer to a serving plate.

2. Cut the mushrooms into uneven chunks and slices to create an interesting texture, and mix all the varieties together. Warm a large, heavy skillet over high heat. Add the mushrooms to the dry pan all at once, then add the olive oil and sprinkle the mixed herbs on top.

3. Cook without stirring for the first 4–5 minutes, allowing the mushrooms to get a brown crust. After 5 minutes, stir to mix in the herbs, and cook until liquid is mostly evaporated.

4. Season mushroom mixture well with lemon juice, salt, and pepper. Spoon onto the grilled bread slices, and garnish with chopped parsley or chives if desired.

Tuscan Baby Artichokes

Serves 4

½ cup olive oil

¼ cup balsamic vinegar

Juice from ½ lemon

½ teaspoon salt

½ teaspoon mustard powder

Fresh ground black or white pepper to taste

Water for boiling

1 teaspoon salt

10 coriander seeds, bruised (optional)

12 baby artichokes, about the size of ping-pong balls

Even though the artichokes are small, they require just as much cooking as large ones do, so practice patience! Grilled artichokes are worth the wait. Add to an antipasto platter along with Spice-Crusted Halloumi Bites (see Chapter 2), green olives, breadsticks, and perhaps some vegetarian deli meat slices.

1. Whisk olive oil, vinegar, lemon juice, ½ teaspoon salt, mustard powder, and pepper together until emulsified.

2. Bring a large pot of water to a boil. Add 1 teaspoon salt and coriander seeds.

3. Trim stems off artichokes and remove outer leaves. Boil the artichokes for 15 minutes, or until barely tender. Drain and allow to cool until they are comfortable to handle.

4. Slice the artichokes in half and use a melon baller to scoop out the choke, the tiny inside leaves that are hair thin.

5. Sprinkle artichokes with balsamic vinaigrette mixture and place on grill over medium heat until lightly browned. Serve hot or cold with the rest of the vinaigrette as a dipping sauce.

Baby Artichokes

Baby artichokes are available in the spring and are a traditional part of Italian Easter celebrations. Double the recipe to serve as a side dish rather than as part of an antipasto platter. Use leftovers (or "planned-overs") in green salads or pasta dishes.

Quesadillas on the Grill

Serves 6

1 red pepper, quartered

2 chili peppers, washed and seeded

½ medium onion, cut into rings

8 corn or 6 flour tortillas

1½ cups shredded cheese (use 2 kinds), such as Cheddar, Muenster, jalapeño jack, or Monterey jack

1 green onion, minced

Fresh ground black pepper to taste

A classic cheesy appetizer filled with red peppers and onions and lightly charred on the grill. For kids, omit the peppers and add in a few squirts of ketchup. They'll love it!

1. Place peppers on grill until skins are darkened. Spread out onion slices and cook until brown grill marks show.

2. Place tortillas on grill for a few seconds, just until warm and flexible, then remove from grill.

3. On ½ of each tortilla, sprinkle an equal amount of each cheese, leaving about 1" around the edges. Add peppers, grilled onion, and minced green onion. Sprinkle with a touch of fresh ground black pepper.

4. Fold in half and place on grill over low or indirect heat. Turn as necessary, about twice in 5 minutes, grilling just until cheese has melted.

Cardamom Naan

Serves 8

1 envelope active dry yeast
1¼ cups lukewarm water (110°F)
1 tablespoon honey
1 tablespoon olive oil, plus more for brushing
3½ cups flour
1 tablespoon salt
1 tablespoon ground cardamom

Naan, Indian flatbread, cooks quickly on the grill, so keep an eye on it. Naan should be soft and pliable, and only lightly crisped.

1. Dissolve yeast in water and stir in honey. Let sit until it becomes foamy (about 10 minutes). Add olive oil, flour, salt, and cardamom and stir until the dough forms into a manageable ball.

2. Place dough on a lightly floured surface and knead until smooth and elastic (about 6 minutes). Divide the dough into 8 equal pieces and shape into balls. Set the balls on an oiled baking sheet and brush with additional olive oil. Cover loosely with plastic and let rise in a warm place until doubled in size (1 to 2 hours).

3. On a lightly floured surface, roll out each ball into an 8" disk. Arrange the disks on oiled baking sheets and let rest for 20 minutes.

4. Brush each naan lightly with olive oil and grill for about 1 minute, until they are golden on the bottom and light bubbles form on the top. Turn and cook until golden all over, about 1 more minute.

Roasted Red Pepper Crostini with Gorgonzola Butter

Yields 12 crostinis

2 red bell peppers, halved, cored, and seeded

¼ cup butter, softened

2 tablespoons Gorgonzola cheese, softened

½ teaspoon celery salt

1 teaspoon red pepper flakes, or to taste

12 1"-thick slices French baguette or artisanal bread

A colorful and flavorful appetizer that goes well with a port wine or a sweet Sauternes.

1. Place peppers on grill over high heat, skin-side down. Grill until charred. Remove the peppers with tongs and place in a paper or heavy plastic bag to cool. When the peppers are cool, peel off the skin and slice the peppers into thin strips.

2. To make the spread, blend together the butter, cheese, celery salt, and red pepper flakes.

3. Grill the bread, and spread a bit of the butter mixture on each toasted piece. Place a small strip of roasted pepper on each crostini.

About Blue Cheese

Gorgonzola is a highly fragrant Italian blue cheese. You may prefer to make this dish using milder French Roquefort, English Stilton, or American Maytag blue cheese—all are delicious and work fine in this dish. The mildest is Danish blue, which is what is usually used in blue cheese salad dressing.

Goat Cheese and Tomato Spread with Roasted Garlic

Serves 12

1 head Roasted Garlic (see Chapter 2)

¼ cup olive oil

1½ tablespoons dried rosemary

1 teaspoon salt

1 tablespoon crushed black peppercorns

5 ounces goat cheese, diced

6 medium tomatoes, diced

2 tablespoons chopped fresh basil

1 loaf French bread

Slivered goat cheese and fresh tomatoes are paired with lightly toasted bread. Look for the freshest, reddest vine-ripened tomatoes you can find for this recipe.

1. Smash roasted garlic until smooth. Combine olive oil with garlic until blended, then add rosemary, salt, and crushed peppercorns.

2. Gently combine garlic-and-oil mixture with goat cheese and tomatoes, then sprinkle with basil. Allow to sit for at least one hour to allow the flavors to develop.

3. To prepare bread, cut into 1"-thick slices and arrange on grill over indirect or low heat. As soon as you have laid down the last slice, turn the first slice, and then the rest in the order in which they were laid down. Once lightly toasted on both sides, remove from grill.

4. Spread the goat cheese mixture on the toasted bread and serve.

Gourmet Grilled Popcorn

Serves 4

3 tablespoons popcorn kernels

3 tablespoons gourmet oil, plus extra for drizzling

½ teaspoon sea salt or kosher salt, or to taste

Get your party started right with dazzling (and noisy!) gourmet grilled popcorn featuring your best gourmet oils. Set out an array of complementing toppers to accompany your popcorn: nutritional yeast or Parmesan cheese (vegan Parmesan for vegans), and lemon pepper, garlic salt, or cayenne for spice.

1. Place popcorn kernels and 2 tablespoons of oil in a foil pie pan. Place another foil pan on top and wrap the seam with aluminum foil to seal shut.

2. Place pan on grill, using tongs to shake it up occasionally. Popcorn will be done after 8–10 minutes.

3. Open foil and drizzle popcorn with extra gourmet oil and sprinkle with salt.

Which Oil to Use?

Corn oil, coconut oil, and a custom "popping oil" are known for their buttery taste and fragrant movie-theater popcorn aromas. But to add a subtle layer of gourmet flavor, use specialty or infused oils. Try avocado oil, chili oil, hazelnut oil, macadamia nut oil, or orange oil, or perhaps a blend. The flavor is subtle, but drizzling a bit more after the popcorn has popped will help make the flavor burst. Easy on the salt—you want to taste the flavors, not the salt! Don't waste your expensive truffle oil in the popping, but do drizzle it on afterwards to really impress.

Avocados with Rémoulade Sauce

Serves 8

1 hard-boiled egg yolk
1 raw egg yolk
1 teaspoon Dijon mustard
Salt and pepper to taste
3 drops Tabasco sauce
1 teaspoon tarragon vinegar
⅔ cup olive oil, chilled
4 avocados, halved and pitted

Grilling avocados softens them and brings out their flavor. A tangy homemade rémoulade sauce is the perfect accompaniment.

1. In a blender or food processor, purée the egg yolks, mustard, salt, pepper, Tabasco, and vinegar. Slowly add the olive oil, blending until thickened.

2. Grill the avocados for 45–50 seconds over low heat, cut-side down. Turn and grill for another 30 seconds. Drizzle generously with sauce and serve.

Fired-Up Salsa Verde

Yields about 1½ cups

1 pound whole green tomatillos, husks removed
2 whole jalapeño peppers
1 small onion, sliced ½" thick
Oil for brushing
2 teaspoons lime juice
⅓ cup fresh cilantro, chopped
2 cloves garlic, chopped
¼ teaspoon sea salt or kosher salt
½ teaspoon sugar (optional)

Store-bought salsas don't even begin to compare to the fresh flavors of a grill-charred homemade version. Don't forget the chips!

1. Brush tomatillos, jalapeños, and onion slices well with oil and place them directly on the grill. Turn once or twice until onions are softened and tomatillos are blackened.

2. Transfer grilled tomatillos, jalapeños, and onions to a food processor and pulse together with remaining ingredients until desired consistency is reached.

Parmesan Garlic Grilled Stuffed Mushrooms

Makes 24 mushrooms

24 button mushrooms, stems removed

2 teaspoons olive oil

4 ounces cream cheese, softened

2 tablespoons chopped chives

¼ cup marinated artichoke hearts, chopped fine

3 tablespoons fresh grated Parmesan cheese

¼ cup seasoned bread crumbs

½ teaspoon parsley

Artichokes and cream cheese fill these little appetizers with plenty of flavor, and grilling adds a lovely, lightly charred crunch.

1. Toss mushrooms with olive oil to coat.

2. In a small bowl, combine cream cheese, chives, and artichoke hearts. In a separate small bowl, combine Parmesan, bread crumbs, and parsley.

3. Spoon cream cheese mixture into mushroom caps, then top with bread crumb mixture.

4. Place on a layer of foil or use a grill basket, and grill for 6–8 minutes.

How to Stuff a Mushroom

Once you've removed the stems, rinse your mushrooms and gently pat dry. If they're organic, you can simply wipe them well with a kitchen cloth to remove any bits of dirt. Using a small spoon, tightly pack the stuffing inside the mushroom cap, heaping it up to form a round mound. The bread crumb topping can also be lightly packed down to prevent the crumbs from falling off.

Chapter 3

Grilled Salads and Meals

Grilled Radicchio with Goat Cheese

Serves 4

4 heads radicchio, chopped in half lengthwise

1 tablespoon olive oil

Salt and fresh ground pepper to taste

2 tablespoons balsamic vinegar (or a balsamic reduction sauce)

¼ cup crumbled goat cheese

Though it's usually thought of as a salad leaf, radicchio, a bittersweet purplish red head lettuce, mellows and becomes pleasantly juicy when it's lightly dressed and cooked on a grill. Don't like balsamic vinegar or goat cheese? Try a drizzle of honey and a crumbled blue cheese instead.

1. Brush radicchio with oil, getting oil in between the leaves, then season with salt and pepper.

2. Place the radicchio cut-side down on a grill over medium heat. Cook until wilting is visible from the sides, for about 2 minutes. Turn to the other cut side and cook for 1 or 2 minutes more, pulling it from the grill before it goes completely limp.

3. Drizzle with balsamic vinegar or a balsamic reduction and crumbled goat cheese.

The Little Purple Lettuce

A cousin of endive, radicchio is known for its tasty bite, a taste similar to mustard greens. If you're not a fan of this bitter bite, tame it with a good soaking in water for 10–15 minutes. You'll need to get it thoroughly dry afterwards before grilling. Another tip? Radicchio is very light, so choose tight round heads that are heavy for their size. While grilling, press them firmly onto the grill rack occasionally.

Summer White Bean and Zucchini Salad

Serves 2 as an entrée or 4 as a side dish

1 clove garlic, minced

1 tablespoon olive oil, plus oil for brushing

1 teaspoon lemon juice

Salt and pepper to taste

1 14-ounce can white beans, drained (cannellini or Great Northern)

¼ cup chopped fresh basil

20 cherry tomatoes

2 zucchinis, chopped into 1"-thick slices

Here's a colorful summer salad that's filling enough for an entrée. Or pair it with a veggie burger. It's a simple salad, so tailor it to your liking. Add in black olives, roasted red pepper, diced red onion, perhaps even some chopped artichoke hearts.

1. Whisk together minced garlic, olive oil, lemon juice, salt, and pepper. Gently toss with the beans in a serving bowl. Adjust seasoning to taste. Place fresh basil on top; do not mix.

2. Lightly brush tomatoes and zucchini with oil, skewer if needed, and grill for just a few minutes on each side, until gently roasted.

3. Immediately place hot zucchini and tomatoes on top of basil, to help release the flavors. Allow to sit for a minute, then gently toss to combine all ingredients.

Baby Corn Caponata

Serves 6

1 small eggplant, sliced ½" thick

1 red or yellow bell pepper, quartered

1 yellow onion, sliced ½" thick

12 ears fresh whole baby corn

4 plum tomatoes

Olive oil for brushing

Salt and pepper to taste

¼ cup basil, chopped

1 tablespoon chopped fresh parsley

¼ cup green olives, sliced

2 tablespoons red wine vinegar

1 tablespoon capers (optional)

Grilled baby corn is bursting with flavors. Here, it sneaks into an otherwise traditional Italian caponata salad with red wine vinegar and capers. Though they're a standard caponata ingredient, capers don't appeal to some people, so omit them if you're not a fan. Don't pass up this recipe just because you can't find fresh baby corn—try canned if you must or just leave them out.

1. Brush the eggplant, bell pepper, onion, corn, and tomatoes with olive oil and season with salt and pepper.

2. Place eggplant, bell pepper, and onion directly on the grill. Skewer tomatoes, then place on grill. Put baby corn in grill basket or wrap in sealed foil packets and place on grill. Grill vegetables for 8–10 minutes or until done.

3. Coarsely chop veggies into strips and gently toss with remaining ingredients.

Grilling Baby Corn

Like its larger cousin, baby corn softens on the grill with a good long soak first. Cover the little ears in water for at least 20 minutes before grilling. If your grill grates are small enough, the corn can go right on the grill. Otherwise, skewer the ears carefully so they don't break, use a grill basket, or wrap in foil oiled with a bit of olive oil.

Spicy Skewered Olive Panzanella

Serves 3

2 tablespoons olive oil

2 tablespoons hot sauce

1 tablespoon water

½ teaspoon garlic powder

¼ teaspoon crushed red pepper flakes

16 1" cubes of crusty Italian or French bread

16 grape tomatoes

16 black olives

16 green olives

1 large red onion, chopped into 16 chunks

Sea salt and fresh ground black pepper to taste

A rustic Italian bread salad, skewered and spiced with hot sauce. These would look nice served over a salad of grilled romaine or baby spinach leaves, but they're perfectly complete standing on their own. Buon appetito!

1. Whisk together the olive oil, hot sauce, water, garlic powder, and red pepper flakes.

2. Gently coat bread cubes, tomatoes, olives, and onions with hot sauce mixture. Skewer, alternating ingredients, then season lightly with salt and pepper.

3. Grill for 3–4 minutes on each side over medium heat, until bread is lightly toasted and vegetables are cooked.

Cold Vietnamese Noodle Salad with Grilled "Chicken"

Serves 4

2 vegan "chicken" cutlets

4 ounces bean thread noodles, softened in hot water for 20 minutes

½ cup thinly sliced scallions

½ cup fresh cilantro leaves

1 to 2 tablespoons crushed red pepper flakes

2 tablespoons lime juice

2 tablespoons soy sauce

1 tablespoon pickled garlic, chopped

Sugar to taste

Here's one way to enjoy a grilled vegetarian "chicken." Both Gardein and Quorn brand cutlets can be placed directly on the grill. Use fresh red chilies instead of the red pepper flakes if you can stand the heat.

1. Grill the vegan chicken cutlets for a few minutes on each side (or according to package instructions) until well marked, then chop into thin strips.

2. Drain the soaked and softened noodles. Combine the noodles, chicken strips, scallions, cilantro leaves, and crushed red pepper flakes in a serving bowl.

3. Mix together the lime juice, soy sauce, pickled garlic, and sugar and toss with the salad ingredients.

Grilled Halloumi with Greek Couscous

Serves 6

1¾ cups water

1½ cups couscous

1 tablespoon olive oil, plus additional for brushing

1 tablespoon lemon juice

2 cloves garlic, minced

1 tablespoon balsamic vinegar

¾ teaspoon oregano

½ cup chopped artichoke hearts

1 recipe Roasted Peppers on the Grill, chopped (see Chapter 5)

Sea salt or kosher salt and fresh ground pepper to taste

1 6-ounce package halloumi cheese, sliced ½" thick

Grilled halloumi tops off a roasted red pepper couscous salad for a Mediterranean-inspired vegetarian entrée. Prepare the rest of the couscous ingredients and have the dish ready to go so that all it needs is the final cheesy touch.

1. Bring water to a boil on the stovetop and add couscous. Turn off heat, cover, and allow to sit for 4–5 minutes, until couscous is cooked and fluffy.

2. Toss prepared couscous with olive oil, lemon juice, garlic, balsamic vinegar, oregano, artichoke hearts, and roasted red peppers. Season generously with salt and fresh ground pepper to taste.

3. Lightly brush halloumi with olive oil, skewer if needed, and grill for about 3 minutes on each side, until generously browned. Add to couscous and serve immediately.

Best Served Hot!

Many cheeses and fine wines may get better with age, but some grilled dishes don't age well. Corn on the cob hot off the grill? Exquisite! The next day? Nothing special. Likewise, grilled halloumi needs to be eaten right away, while it's still hot and melty. If your halloumi becomes cool and rubbery, just rewarm it up on the grill for a few minutes over low or indirect heat.

Southwestern Barbecue Tofu Salad

Serves 4

1 16-ounce package firm or extra-firm tofu, well pressed and sliced ¾" thick

⅓ cup plus ¼ cup barbecue sauce, divided

1 15-ounce can corn kernels, drained, or kernels from 2 ears fresh grilled corn

1 red bell pepper, chopped small

1 avocado, diced (optional)

1 large head romaine or iceberg lettuce, coarsely chopped

2 tablespoons chopped fresh cilantro

3 tablespoons vegan mayonnaise

1–2 tablespoons water (as needed)

In a hurry? Use a preflavored store-bought tofu and skip the marinating time. For extra crunch, crumble a handful of tortilla chips on top just before serving.

1. Marinate tofu in ⅓ cup barbecue sauce for 10–15 minutes.

2. Grill tofu for a few minutes on each side, basting occasionally with additional barbecue sauce.

3. In a large serving bowl, combine corn kernels, red bell pepper, avocado, lettuce, and cilantro.

4. Chop tofu into cubes and add to bowl.

5. In a separate small bowl, whisk together mayonnaise and ¼ cup barbecue sauce, adding water as needed to get the desired consistency. Dress salad with sauce, tossing gently to combine.

Balsamic-Brushed Endive with Shaved Parmesan

Serves 4

4 heads endive

Oil for brushing

Salt and fresh ground pepper to taste

1 tablespoon balsamic vinegar

1 teaspoon Dijon mustard

Fresh Parmesan (optional)

Use seasoned bread crumbs as a finisher instead of the Parmesan shavings if you're grilling for vegans.

1. Slice endive heads in half lengthwise and brush both sides with oil. Season lightly with salt and pepper.

2. Grill, cut-side down, for 8–10 minutes, turning once.

3. Whisk together balsamic and Dijon and drizzle over grilled endive. Top each grilled endive with a few curls of shaved Parmesan.

Grilled Vegetable Tabbouleh

Serves 4

2½ cups water

1 cup bulgur wheat

3 tablespoons lemon juice

3 tablespoons olive oil, divided

2 cloves garlic, minced

¼ cup fresh parsley, minced

¼ cup fresh mint, minced

3 scallions, chopped

1 zucchini, chopped

1 yellow squash, chopped

1 large tomato, chopped

Salt and pepper to taste

¼ cup toasted pine nuts (optional)

Make the tabbouleh salad ahead of time, topping it off with the grilled veggies on grilling day. For tabbouleh, if you're going to skewer the veggies to grill them, dice them to about ½" cubes. If you're going to use a grill basket instead of skewers, dice the veggies finely.

1. Bring water to a boil on the stovetop. Add bulgur wheat, stirring to combine well. Reduce heat to a slow simmer, cover, and cook for 8–10 minutes or according to package instructions, until liquid is absorbed and bulgur has cooked. Cool.

2. Combine cooled bulgur with lemon juice, 2 tablespoons olive oil, garlic, parsley, mint, and scallions.

3. Toss zucchini, yellow squash, and tomato chunks with 1 tablespoon olive oil; skewer, and grill until soft.

4. To serve, add grilled vegetables to bulgur, or serve skewers on top. Season with extra salt and pepper to taste, and garnish with pine nuts, if desired.

Sesame Shiitakes with Bok Choy and Soba

Serves 4

1 12-ounce package soba noodles

⅓ cup rice vinegar

3 tablespoons sesame oil

1½ tablespoons soy sauce

½ teaspoon red pepper flakes

4 shiitake mushrooms, stems removed

2 heads baby bok choy, chopped in half

Salt and pepper

¼ cup chopped scallions (optional)

Sure, portobellos may steal the show as the superstars of the grill, but shiitakes deserve recognition for coming in a close second. Garnish this chilled Asian noodle salad with sesame seeds or grated ginger. Serve with a dab of wasabi on the side for your adventurous guests.

1. Simmer soba noodles in water until soft, about 4–5 minutes. Drain, then rinse under cold water. Chill until completely cooled, at least 30 minutes.

2. Whisk together the rice vinegar, sesame oil, soy sauce, and red pepper flakes. Brush mushrooms and bok choy well with sauce, and sprinkle lightly with salt and pepper.

3. Grill on a well-greased grill, about 5–6 minutes, turning once or twice. Bok choy may be done before the mushrooms. Reserve extra basting sauce.

4. Toss extra basting sauce with cooled soba noodles and scallions. Coarsely chop the bok choy and shiitake, and plate on top of prepared soba noodles.

Caution!

Not all soba noodles are vegan; some contain egg. If you're cooking for vegans, best to read the label to make sure, or, use another Asian-style noodle, such as rice vermicelli or udon, or even just plain spaghetti.

Red, White, and Yellow Pasta Tricolore

Serves 4

1 recipe Roasted Peppers on the Grill (see Chapter 5)

2 roasted yellow bell peppers

1 tablespoon lemon juice

3 tablespoons olive oil

½ teaspoon red pepper flakes

½ teaspoon garlic salt, or to taste

16 ounces pasta, cooked

⅓ cup fresh chopped basil

8 ounces fresh mozzarella, chopped, or 8 1-ounce balls, halved

This understated yet delicious recipe is just waiting for you to personalize it with diced avocado, a few shakes of Italian seasoning, perhaps even some green olives, a handful of pine nuts, or a touch of champagne vinegar. For a warm entrée, select a large thick pasta, such as penne or rigatoni; for cold pasta salad, use small shells or bowties.

1. Chop roasted peppers into thin strips.

2. Whisk together the lemon juice, olive oil, red pepper flakes, and garlic salt. Gently toss with cooked pasta.

3. Combine dressed pasta, pepper strips, basil, and mozzarella. Serve hot or chilled.

Greek Watermelon and Grilled Halloumi Salad

Serves 6

1 6-ounce package halloumi cheese, sliced into ½"-thick cubes

1 red onion, chopped

Oil for brushing

4 cups watermelon, cubed

½ cup sliced black olives

2 teaspoons balsamic vinegar

Salt and pepper to taste

When it's hot in Greece, cooks pair watermelon and halloumi cheese for a cooling snack. When it's hot in your backyard, try this vibrant red-and-white Greek-inspired salad.

1. Brush halloumi and red onion with oil, then skewer and grill for a few minutes on each side until cheese is well browned.

2. Remove cheese and onions from skewers and quickly toss with remaining ingredients.

3. Season lightly with salt and pepper to taste. Serve immediately.

Variations on a Theme

Add strawberries and pine nuts and toss with baby spinach to turn this Greek treat into a colorful salad. Or, for the 4th of July, add a handful of blueberries to transform this salad into a red, white, and blue masterpiece.

Grilled Asparagus with Baby Spinach in Mustard Vinaigrette

Serves 3

¼ cup olive oil, plus 2 tablespoons, divided

2 tablespoons Dijon mustard

2 tablespoons apple cider vinegar

1 shallot, minced

1 teaspoon sugar

1 pound asparagus, trimmed

Salt and pepper to taste

1 6-ounce bag baby spinach

Shaved or grated Parmesan (optional)

A tangy and sweet mustard vinaigrette dresses this savory green dish. Asparagus is one of the superstars of the grill, but it needs little flavor enhancement to shine.

1. Make a mustard vinaigrette by whisking or blending together the ¼ cup olive oil, the Dijon mustard, cider vinegar, minced shallot, and sugar. Set aside.

2. Toss asparagus with 2 tablespoons olive oil to coat, then season well with salt and pepper.

3. If needed, skewer the asparagus across the bottom and again, halfway up. Over medium to low heat, grill for about 8–10 minutes per side, depending on the heat of the grill and the thickness of the spears.

4. Plate asparagus over a bed of baby spinach leaves. Drizzle with dressing and garnish with shaved or grated Parmesan, if desired.

French Fennel, Basil, and Tomato Salad

Serves 4

2 medium fennel bulbs, trimmed and cut into quarters

16 cherry tomatoes

½ cup French dressing

2 tablespoons olive oil

10 fresh basil leaves

Although these vegetables are threaded onto separate skewers, they make a marvelous combination when put together and tossed with olive oil.

1. Parboil the fennel chunks in salted water for 10 minutes. Drain the fennel on paper towels. Thread the tomatoes and fennel onto separate skewers. Brush with French dressing.

2. Place the fennel over medium heat and cook for 4 minutes per side, or until browned. Put the tomatoes on the grill just after you turn the fennel. The tomatoes will cook more quickly than the fennel.

3. Remove the vegetables from skewers and place the vegetables on a platter. Sprinkle with olive oil and basil, and serve either warm or cooled.

Grilled Pear and Romaine Salad

Serves 4

2 hearts of romaine, well cleaned

Olive oil for brushing

Dash salt and fresh ground pepper, divided

2 pears, sliced thin

¼ cup dried cranberries (or dried blueberries or cherries)

⅓ cup candied pecans, coarsely chopped

⅓ cup cranberry juice concentrate, thawed

3 tablespoons red wine vinegar

½ teaspoon sugar

½ teaspoon Dijon mustard

With cranberries and candied nuts, this grilled pear salad has more of a wintry feel, but the grilled flavor makes it a summer treat! You can use store-bought vinaigrette, but choose something fruity, like raspberry.

1. Cut romaine in half lengthwise. Drizzle the cut side with olive oil and add just a touch of salt and pepper. Grill, cut-side down, for 2 minutes.

2. Place pears on a well-greased grill and heat for 2–3 minutes on each side.

3. Coarsely chop grilled romaine. Toss in a serving bowl or platter with cranberries and pecans. Place pears on top.

4. Whisk or blend together the remaining ingredients to form a dressing and drizzle on top of pears and romaine.

Let the Smoke Shine on Through

Grilling the romaine is optional, but it only takes an extra minute, and lends a slight smokiness to this textured salad. Warming up the dressing a bit first adds another surprising layer of flavor, so heat it up for a couple of seconds, too. You want the dressing just warmed, not hot. One final tip: go easy on the dressing, as you don't want to overpower the naturally fantastic flavors of the grilled pears and romaine.

Easy Roasted Vegetable Pasta

Serves 12

1 recipe Grilled Vegetable Antipasto (see Chapter 5), chopped into 1" pieces

1 pound fusilli, penne, or other small pasta shape, cooked

2 tablespoons olive oil

2 teaspoons balsamic vinegar

Pinch of sugar

1 teaspoon kosher salt

¼ teaspoon fresh ground black pepper

½ cup parsley, coarsely chopped

This recipe combines an American backyard barbecue with a summer picnic in Northern Italy. Cook the pasta all the way to soft (past "al dente") for this pasta salad.

1. Place grilled vegetables in a bowl, and allow them to come to room temperature.

2. Add the cooked pasta, olive oil, vinegar, and sugar. Toss to coat. Let stand 30 minutes.

3. Season with salt and pepper and toss with parsley.

Roasted Tomato and Cucumber Salad

Serves 3

1¼ pounds plum tomatoes

1 tablespoon oil

1 cucumber, peeled and diced

1½ teaspoons red wine vinegar

1 tablespoon fresh dill, chopped

½ teaspoon salt

¼ teaspoon pepper

1½ teaspoons lemon juice

This salad is equally good fresh and warm off the grill or as chilled leftovers the next day. Serve it over a bed of lettuce, if you'd like.

1. Roast tomatoes on grill until skins start to blacken. Remove from grill and peel off skins.

2. In a large mixing bowl, combine tomatoes with remaining ingredients. Mix well, breaking up tomatoes while stirring.

Lemon Couscous with Grilled Persimmons

Serves 4

1¾ cups water or vegetable broth

1½ cups couscous

⅓ cup chopped green onions

⅓ cup raisins or currants

1 8-ounce container plain, lemon, or vanilla nondairy yogurt

1 tablespoon fresh lemon juice

2 teaspoons Dijon mustard

4 Fuyu persimmons, sliced into thick wedges

Oil for brushing

Salt and fresh ground pepper

California meets the Middle East in this light summery meal perfect for warm afternoons. Pair with a light-bodied sparkling wine, or a fruity white, such as a Sauvignon Blanc or a Riesling.

1. Bring water or vegetable broth to a boil and add couscous. Turn off heat, cover, and allow to sit for 4–5 minutes, until couscous is cooked and fluffy. Add green onions and raisins.

2. Whisk together the yogurt, lemon juice, and mustard, and combine with cooked couscous.

3. Brush persimmons well with oil or gently toss to coat. Season very lightly with just a touch of salt and pepper.

4. Place on the grill for 4–5 minutes, turning once. Plate grilled persimmons on top of prepared couscous and season with extra salt and pepper to taste.

Grilled Fennel with Citrus Vinaigrette

Serves 4

3 tablespoons fresh-squeezed orange juice

1 tablespoon balsamic vinegar

2 tablespoons olive oil

2 bulbs fennel, chopped into 1"-thick rounds

Olive oil for brushing

Salt and pepper to taste

1 head romaine, coarsely chopped

2 mandarin oranges, peeled and segmented

½ red onion, thinly sliced (optional)

When grilled, the strong licorice taste of fennel fades to a pleasantly earthy undertone that pairs nicely with a citrus vinaigrette. Dried cranberries or slivered almonds go well with this salad.

1. To make vinaigrette, whisk together orange juice and balsamic vinegar, slowly adding in olive oil until emulsified and thick.

2. Brush fennel bulbs lightly with olive oil on both sides, and season generously with salt and pepper. Grill for 6–8 minutes, turning once.

3. Toss fennel slices with romaine, mandarin orange segments, onions, and vinaigrette, or plate attractively over a bed of lettuce and drizzle with vinaigrette. Season again with salt and pepper to taste.

Vegetarian Caesar with Grilled Tofu

Serves 8

2 blocks firm or extra-firm tofu, well pressed

Salt and fresh ground pepper to taste

1 egg yolk

1 tablespoon Dijon mustard

2 tablespoons lemon juice

2 cloves garlic, minced

½ cup peanut oil (or vegetable oil)

¼ cup grated fresh Parmesan cheese, plus extra for garnish

1 large head romaine lettuce, coarsely chopped

1 cup croutons

Use a store-bought mock chicken if you prefer it to grilled tofu. Be sure to use fresh Parmesan cheese.

1. Season the tofu with salt and pepper on both sides, then cook on a well-greased grill until golden brown, about 5–6 minutes on each side. Chop into 1" cubes.

2. In a mixing bowl or food processor, combine the egg yolk, mustard, lemon juice, and garlic. Then vigorously whisk or process in the oil, starting just a drop at a time, gradually drizzling it in a small stream, until all is emulsified into a smooth mayonnaise. Stir in the ¼ cup cheese.

3. Toss the lettuce with the dressing, and divide onto 8 plates, arranging tofu and croutons on top. For garnish, shave a couple of curls of fresh Parmesan onto each salad, using a vegetable peeler.

Crunchy Croutons

Virtually any bread can be seasoned and toasted to make crunchy croutons—perfect for sprucing up soups and salads, or just for snacking. Here's how: Cut some leftover bread into bite-sized pieces and toss it into in a large bowl with a generous coating of oil, a bit of salt, and some Italian seasonings, garlic powder, a dash of cayenne, or whatever you prefer. Transfer to a baking sheet and bake 15–20 minutes at 275°F, tossing once or twice, until croutons are crisp all the way through and starting to brown at the corners.

Portobello Stuffed with Summer Orzo

Serves 4

1 cup cooked orzo

1 cup corn kernels

1 large tomato, diced

¼ cup chopped scallions

1 tablespoon lemon juice

2 teaspoons olive oil, plus additional for brushing

1 teaspoon red wine vinegar

Salt and fresh ground black pepper to taste

4 large Portobello mushrooms

These stuffed mushrooms are like little individual mini-casseroles. Pile on the orzo as high as possible, and go ahead—have two!

1. Combine orzo with corn kernels, tomato, and scallions, then toss with lemon juice, 2 teaspoons olive oil, and red wine vinegar. Season well with salt and pepper.

2. Brush portobellos with extra olive oil. Heat grill to medium and grill portobellos for 3 minutes, turn, then grill for 3–4 more minutes. Give larger mushrooms an extra minute or two.

3. Remove mushrooms from grill and fill with orzo mixture, piling as high as possible. Return to the grill to warm for 1–2 minutes.

Mediterranean Skewers with Kalamata and Feta Couscous

Serves 4

2 tablespoons lemon juice

2 tablespoons white wine

¼ cup olive oil

1 shallot, minced

1 teaspoon oregano

½ teaspoon red pepper flakes

¼ teaspoon salt, plus extra for garnish

⅛ teaspoon pepper, plus extra for garnish

16 cherry tomatoes

1 red bell pepper, cut into chunks

12 button mushrooms

1¾ cups water

1½ cups couscous

¼ cup feta cheese, crumbled

¼ cup kalamata olives, sliced

Greek-flavored skewers are served with couscous dressed with feta and olives. Omit the feta for your vegan friends, and add a couple of shakes of vegan Parmesan or nutritional yeast instead.

1. Whisk together the lemon juice, wine, olive oil, shallot, oregano, red pepper flakes, salt, and pepper. Add tomatoes, bell pepper, and mushrooms and allow to marinate for at least 30 minutes. Drain and reserve extra marinade.

2. Bring water to a boil and add couscous. Turn off heat, cover, and allow to sit for 4–5 minutes, until couscous is cooked and fluffy. Toss couscous with reserved marinade, then add feta and kalamata olives.

3. Skewer tomatoes, bell peppers, and mushrooms. Grill for a few minutes until well roasted.

4. To serve, plate skewers on top of couscous and sprinkle with an extra dash of salt and pepper.

Chapter 4

Reinventing the Barbecue Classics

Papas Asadas with Salsa Verde

Serves 2

1 large baking potato

¼ cup Fired-Up Salsa Verde (see recipe in Chapter 2) or green enchilada sauce

2 tablespoons grated cheese (Monterey jack, Cheddar, or a Mexican blend)

8 jalapeño slices, fresh or jarred

Serve these simple stuffed potatoes with a side of sour cream and some mariachi music. I recommend Herb Alpert and the Tijuana Brass.

1. Parboil potatoes until just barely tender, about 6–8 minutes. Slice in half and remove enough of the cooked potato flesh to make a shell, reserving the flesh.

2. Combine the reserved potato flesh with the salsa verde and return to potato shells. Sprinkle with cheese and top with jalapeño slices.

3. Return potatoes to grill for 3–4 minutes, or until cheese has melted.

Easy Grilled Seitan

Eggplant Pizza Rounds

Indian-Spiced Polenta with
Mango Chutney

Southwestern Barbecue Tofu Salad

Texas Caviar

Coconut-Glazed Pineapple

Peach Cinnamon Crisp

Wild Rice Salad with Apples and Almonds

Easy Sweet Indonesian Seitan Satay

Cold Vietnamese Noodle Salad with Grilled Vegetarian "Chicken"

Tofu and Pesto
Panini on Ciabatta

Tempeh "Chicken"
Salad Sandwich

Maple Dijon Sweet Potatoes

Serves 4

3 large sweet potatoes

3 tablespoons maple syrup

3 tablespoons Dijon mustard

½ teaspoon garlic powder

½ teaspoon onion powder

¼ teaspoon salt

⅛ teaspoon black pepper

Dash cayenne pepper (optional)

Olive oil for brushing

You really can't go wrong no matter what you do with sweet potatoes on the grill. This isn't meant to be a spicy recipe, so don't go overboard on the cayenne pepper—you want just enough to make the other flavors pop.

1. Slice sweet potatoes about 1" thick. Boil water in a large saucepan on the stovetop. Reduce heat and simmer sweet potatoes for 6–8 minutes. Remove from heat and rinse in cold water.

2. Whisk together maple syrup and Dijon mustard, then set aside. In a separate small bowl, combine garlic powder, onion powder, salt, pepper, and cayenne. Brush sweet potato slices with olive oil, then coat with spice mixture.

3. Brush both sides of sweet potato slices well with maple-Dijon glaze and place on grill over medium heat. Grill for 2–3 minutes, then turn, brush again with glaze, and heat for 1–2 more minutes.

Sun-Dried Tomato Corn on the Cob

Serves 4

½ stick (¼ cup) butter or margarine, softened

1 tablespoon chopped fresh parsley

1 tablespoon chopped fresh basil

2 tablespoons sun-dried tomato pesto

Dash sea salt or kosher salt

4 ears fresh corn

Your friends will think you're a trained gourmet when you whip up this simple herbed sauce for summer sweet corn. The added basil and parsley freshen up the jarred pesto. Slather it on thick, and savor each bite.

1. Combine softened butter with parsley, basil, pesto, and salt.
2. Grill corn and spread generously with pesto butter just before serving.

Grilling Corn

Otherwise rational people have serious disagreements about how to grill corn. Some people prefer to presoak it without disturbing the husks. Others do a delicate operation, folding back the husks, removing the silk, adding salt and butter, then tying the husks back over the corn. Still others peel the corn, spread butter on it, and put it directly on the grill naked. Still others prefer their corn wrapped in foil and placed directly on the coals. Take your pick of methods, or try them all.

Garlic-Free Parmesan Basil Bread

Serves 8

¼ cup unsalted butter

1 teaspoon dried oregano, crumbled

1 teaspoon dried basil, crumbled

Fresh ground black pepper

Celery salt to taste

1 cup fresh Parmesan cheese, grated

1 loaf Italian bread

Garlic-haters out there can try this grilled Parmesan bread recipe, which is similar to a garlic bread but without the garlic.

1. In a small saucepan over low heat, mix together the butter, oregano, basil, pepper, celery salt, and cheese. Heat until the butter melts, mixing constantly.

2. Cut the bread in half lengthwise, then score crosswise so that guests can break off chunks. Don't cut all the way through.

3. Brush the butter-and-herb mixture onto the bread. Wrap the whole loaf in aluminum foil and grill over medium heat for 8–10 minutes. Garnish with additional fresh herbs or Parmesan, if desired.

Paprika and Mustard Steak Fries

Serves 4

4 medium potatoes

1 tablespoon paprika

2 teaspoons chili powder

½ teaspoon mustard powder

½ teaspoon garlic powder

½ teaspoon salt

¼ teaspoon cayenne pepper, or to taste

1 tablespoon olive oil

Yes, vegetarians love steak fries, too. Pair them with a veggie burger and a cold beer, and don't forget the ketchup. Or mayonnaise, if you're Australian. This recipe works equally well with sweet potatoes.

1. Parboil potatoes until just barely tender, about 6–8 minutes. Rinse under cool water. When cool enough to handle, chop into thick wedges.

2. Combine paprika, chili powder, mustard powder, garlic powder, salt, and cayenne in a small bowl. Lightly brush or toss potato wedges with olive oil, then coat well with spice blend.

3. Place on grill over medium heat for 5–7 minutes, turning once.

Pesto Potato Salad

Serves 4

2 pounds potatoes, any kind, chopped into 1" chunks

2 tablespoons olive oil

3 tablespoons pesto

¼ cup mayonnaise

1 teaspoon Dijon mustard

¼ cup chopped green onions

Salt and pepper to taste

It's an unspoken rule that when food is eaten outdoors, potato salad must be on the menu. But there's no rule that says potato salad has to be boring. A touch of crumbled feta or a skewer or two of grilled cherry tomatoes further enliven this pesto potato salad.

1. Place chopped potatoes on a large sheet of foil. Drizzle generously with olive oil, then wrap and grill potatoes for 25–30 minutes, until potatoes are done.

2. Mix pesto with mayonnaise and Dijon. Toss with grilled potatoes and green onions. Season lightly with salt and pepper to taste.

Working with Foil

Anytime you wrap anything in foil and place it on the grill—whether it's potatoes, beets, corn, or carrots—be very careful when opening it up. The steam inside foil packets can be surprisingly hot, even when the outer foil layers are cool enough to handle.

Salty Sweet Kettle Corn

Serves 4

2 tablespoons soy sauce

2 teaspoons brown sugar

2 tablespoons vegan margarine, gently melted

4 ears fresh corn on the cob, husks removed

Do you like the salty-sweet combination of kettle popcorn? This recipe turns fresh corn into kettle popcorn's grilled twin. If it gets a bit messy, don't be shy about licking your fingers.

1. Whisk together the soy sauce, brown sugar, and melted vegan margarine until combined.

2. Place corn directly on the grill for 3–4 minutes. Brush corn with sugared margarine mixture and heat another 3–4 minutes.

3. Brush corn again with sugared margarine mixture just before serving.

Curry Masala Corn on the Cob

Serves 4

2 teaspoons curry powder

1 teaspoon cumin

¾ teaspoon salt

4 ears corn

¼ cup vegan margarine

Get your (clean) hands dirty by really rubbing this spice mixture on the kernels.

1. Combine the curry powder, cumin, and salt.

2. Rub about half the vegan margarine on the corn. Then rub the spice mix on the corn.

3. Grill until tender, about 5–6 minutes per side, turning often. Rub again with margarine and spice mixture just before serving.

Classic Garlic Bread

Serves 3

1 small loaf French bread

½ cup olive oil

4 cloves garlic, minced

Fresh ground black pepper to taste

¼ teaspoon onion salt

3 tablespoons butter or margarine, melted

1 teaspoon chopped parsley, fresh or dried

Pick out a small loaf of French bread, about 6" long, for this all-American grilled side. For maximum flavor, be sure to apply the butter mixture liberally between the slices.

1. Cut the bread into 1"-thick slices without cutting all the way through each slice.

2. Combine the remaining ingredients in a mixing bowl and stir well. Using a basting brush, apply to both sides of each bread slice without separating the slices too far.

3. Wrap the entire loaf in aluminum foil and set on the grill over medium heat. Turn after 4–6 minutes and heat for another 4–6 minutes.

Sweet Potato Pie on a Stick

Serves 4

3 medium sweet potatoes, chopped into 1" chunks

¼ cup butter or margarine, melted

1 tablespoon maple syrup

1 tablespoon brown sugar

¾ teaspoon vanilla extract

½ teaspoon cinnamon

¼ teaspoon nutmeg

Sweetened condensed milk (optional)

This Southern classic on a stick is ridiculously delicious when drizzled with sweetened condensed milk. To encourage the milk to drizzle better, warm the tin in hot water for a few minutes.

1. Simmer sweet potato chunks in water for 5–6 minutes to soften. Drain, then place on skewers.

2. In a small bowl, combine melted butter, maple syrup, brown sugar, vanilla, cinnamon, and nutmeg.

3. Baste sweet potatoes with butter–maple syrup glaze. Place potatoes on grill over medium heat for 5–7 minutes, turning once or twice and basting with extra glaze.

4. Drizzle with a bit of sweetened condensed milk and serve.

Rosemary Grilled Potatoes

Serves 4

4 medium potatoes, chopped into 1" chunks
1 small onion, chopped (optional)
2–3 cloves garlic, minced
3 tablespoons olive oil
2 tablespoons rosemary, coarsely chopped, plus unchopped sprigs for garnish
Salt and pepper to taste

Rosemary and potatoes are a classic culinary combination, and this recipe takes it outdoors for a simple herbal side dish. For a bit of aromatherapy while you're guarding the grill, place a few sprigs of fresh rosemary right on the coals.

1. In a large bowl, combine all ingredients, coating potatoes.
2. Place potato mixture on a large piece of foil. Wrap and seal tightly.
3. Grill foil packet 30–35 minutes, turning once. Garnish with additional fresh rosemary sprigs.

Trimming Extra Fat

You're eating vegetarian—you've already trimmed lots of extra fat from your diet! In foil packet recipes such as this one, the olive oil serves a double purpose. Yes, it adds a bit of extra flavor, but it also prevents the ingredients from sticking to the foil. To cut the olive oil from foil packet recipes, use a nonstick spray to coat the foil before placing your ingredients in the middle and wrapping.

Kalamata Buttered Corn on the Cob

Makes ½ cup butter

3 tablespoons kalamata, niçoise, or other black olives, pitted

½ cup (1 stick) unsalted butter, room temperature

1½ teaspoon fresh-squeezed lemon juice

Pinch red pepper flakes (optional)

4 ears fresh corn on the cob, husks removed

Americana icon Garrison Keillor once said, "Sex is good, but not as good as fresh, sweet corn." Try this recipe with fresh, local, organic summer corn, then decide whether or not he was kidding. This recipe makes plenty, so plan on having leftover kalamata butter to spread on lightly grilled artisan bread.

1. In a food processor, pulse together the olives and butter, then the lemon juice and red pepper flakes. Scrape down the sides of the bowl with a rubber spatula and mix a little by hand as needed.

2. Grill corn on medium, 6–8 minutes, turning occasionally.

3. Rub olive butter onto hot grilled corn and serve.

Potatoes with Yellow Curry Sauce

Makes 8 stuffed potato halves

4 potatoes

½ cup plain yogurt

2 teaspoons lime juice

2 teaspoons curry powder

½ teaspoon cumin

½ teaspoon garlic powder

¼ teaspoon salt

¼ cup chopped green onions (optional)

While the curry may have Indian roots, this combination of ingredients is more of a British invention. Thick Greek yogurt works best, but you could also use sour cream or a vegan substitute for your dairy-free friends.

1. Parboil potatoes until just barely tender, about 6–8 minutes. Rinse under cool water. When cool enough to handle, slice in half and scoop out enough of the cooked potato flesh to form a shell, reserving the flesh.

2. Whisk together the yogurt, lime juice, curry powder, cumin, garlic powder, and salt.

3. Combine potato flesh with ½ of yogurt-curry mixture and place in potato shells. Wrap well in foil, then grill until heated through, 4–5 minutes.

4. Carefully open foil and place a generous dollop of remaining yogurt-curry sauce on top of each potato. Garnish with green onions, if desired.

Gourmet Truffled Garlic Bread

Serves 8

1 16-ounce loaf French or other artisan bread

¼ cup (½ stick) vegan margarine, softened

2 tablespoons truffle oil, plus an additional 2 tablespoons for drizzling

¼ teaspoon sea salt or kosher salt

4 cloves garlic, minced

This garlic bread recipe keeps it simple to let the flavors of the truffle oil shine through. After all, you paid good money for the truffle oil, so you want to really taste it!

1. Cut the bread into 1"-thick slices without cutting all the way through the slices.

2. Combine the softened margarine with 2 tablespoons truffle oil, salt, and garlic, mixing well. Spread truffle-oil-margarine evenly on the bread, making sure it gets in between the slices.

3. Wrap the bread in aluminum foil and place on the grill over medium-low heat for 3–4 minutes, turning once, just until warmed and lightly toasted. Drizzle with extra truffle oil just before serving.

Cheesy Cheddar Sweet Potatoes

Serves 4

4 medium sweet potatoes
Oil for brushing
Butter or margarine to taste
Salt and pepper to taste
½ cup sharp Cheddar cheese, grated

Grilling makes these sweet potatoes succulent, smoky, and sweet.

1. Scrub sweet potatoes and brush lightly with oil. Place whole sweet potatoes on squares of aluminum foil and wrap tightly.

2. Place on hot grill and cook for 45 minutes to 1 hour, turning occasionally.

3. Remove from heat and slice lengthwise through both foil and potato with a sharp knife. Serve with butter, salt, and pepper. Top with cheese and serve hot.

Red Curry Corn on the Cob

Serves 4

2 tablespoons coconut cream (coconut milk will work for a lighter version)
2 tablespoons Thai red curry paste
½ teaspoon lime juice
½ teaspoon salt
4 ears fresh summer corn

Corn is a popular treat for kids at outdoor markets and temple fairs in Thailand. The kernels are served in a cup, swimming in margarine and sugar. This nontraditional yet still Thai-inspired recipe is much healthier, with no hydrogenated oils. Check the ingredients to make sure your jarred curry paste is vegan.

1. Whisk together the coconut cream, curry paste, lime juice, and salt until mixed.

2. Slather the coconut mixture on the corn and grill 6–8 minutes, basting with extra sauce and turning occasionally. Brush with sauce again just before serving.

Not the Season?

Grilled corn recipes with strong flavors, such as this one, can mask less-than-perfect corn. If your local varieties are of inferior quality, or it's just not the season, this is a good recipe to try, along with Kalamata Buttered Corn on the Cob (see Chapter 4) and Fiery Chipotle Butter Corn on the Cob (see Chapter 4). Soak the corn first for 20–30 minutes, with husks removed, to help tenderize a tough out-of-season ear.

Scallions and Potatoes with Catalonian Romesco

Serves 4

1 cup chopped roasted red peppers

⅓ cup sliced almonds

¾ teaspoon garlic powder

1 tablespoon red wine or sherry vinegar

1 slice bread

½ teaspoon paprika

¼ teaspoon red pepper flakes (optional)

2–3 tablespoons olive oil

4 medium baking potatoes

Olive oil for brushing

Salt and fresh ground pepper to taste

½ teaspoon sage

1 bunch green onions

A heavenly roasted red pepper Romesco sauce goes perfectly with an earthy roasted potato. The scallions and sauce are reminiscent of Catalonian grills in Spain, but the baked potato is all-American. Serve it with a sparkling Spanish cava or a down-home American brewski.

1. Using a blender or food processor, process together the roasted red peppers, almonds, garlic powder, red wine, bread, paprika, and red pepper flakes. Slowly add olive oil, adding just enough to get the sauce smooth. Romesco sauce should be thick.

2. Cover potatoes in water and boil for 6–8 minutes, until tender. Drain.

3. Once cooled, chop potatoes in half and coat with olive oil, then season generously with salt, pepper, and sage. Place cut-side down and grill for 3–4 minutes, until lightly charred.

4. Brush green onions with olive oil, season lightly with salt and pepper, and place directly on the grill, skewering if needed. Heat for just a minute or two until lightly wilted. Remove from grill and chop coarsely.

5. Top potatoes with a generous portion of Romesco sauce and grilled green onions.

Rosemary Grilled Garlic Bread

Serves 8

1 16-ounce loaf French or other artisan bread
1 bulb Roasted Garlic (see Chapter 2)
3 tablespoons vegan margarine, softened
2 tablespoons fresh rosemary, coarsely chopped
½ teaspoon sea salt or kosher salt
1 tablespoon olive oil

Use fresh homegrown rosemary for this recipe. What's that? You don't grow your own rosemary? Why not? Rosemary is easy to grow on your kitchen windowsill, or in your backyard or patio garden!

1. Cut bread into 1" slices, not cutting all the way through each slice.

2. Mash roasted garlic bulb with softened margarine to form a paste. Spread over sliced bread.

3. Sprinkle evenly with rosemary and salt, then drizzle with olive oil.

4. Wrap in foil and grill over medium heat for 6–8 minutes.

Orange Sweet Potatoes

Serves 4

4 large sweet potatoes
Water for boiling
½ cup vegan margarine, melted
3 tablespoons brown sugar
1 tablespoon orange juice

Try this recipe with purple yams for an exotic and colorful dish.

1. Cut unpeeled sweet potatoes into 1"-thick slices. Bring a large pot of water to a boil and add the slices. Cook until the potatoes just begin to soften, about 5–6 minutes. Cool and peel.

2. In a small mixing bowl, combine margarine, brown sugar, and orange juice.

3. Place sweet potato slices on grill over medium heat and brush with margarine mixture. Grill, turning once, until well browned, basting occasionally with extra margarine-and-orange-juice mix.

Wasabi Avocado Cream Potatoes

Serves 4

4 medium baking potatoes, coarsely chopped

1 tablespoon olive oil

1 teaspoon wasabi paste (or powder, mixed with water)

1 avocado, mashed

¼ cup vegan mayonnaise

This recipe works particularly well with bland potatoes—save the Yukon gold and heirloom baby blues for a recipe that doesn't call for them to be overpowered with one of the strongest flavors on the planet. If you like wasabi, double or triple the amount given here.

1. Place potatoes on a large sheet of foil and drizzle with olive oil. Wrap tightly in foil and place on grill for 30–35 minutes.

2. Mash together the wasabi, avocado, and mayonnaise. Spoon on top of grilled potatoes.

Got Leftovers?

Leftover grilled potatoes always make a wonderfully smoky potato salad the next day, and these wasabi potatoes are no exception. For a spicy green wasabi potato salad, coarsely chop the cooked potatoes and gently toss with the leftover wasabi cream. Add a bit of extra mayonnaise, chopped scallions, vegetarian bacon bits, a sprinkle of salt, and a handful of chopped onions or celery.

Fiery Chipotle Butter Corn on the Cob

Serves 4

¼ cup vegan margarine

2 teaspoons minced chipotle in adobo

½ teaspoon adobo sauce

½ teaspoon lime juice

Cayenne pepper to taste

¼ teaspoon salt

4 ears fresh corn on the cob

If you like your corn on the cob spicy, you'll love this recipe, which doubles up the fire by using both chipotles and cayenne.

1. Heat margarine and chipotle in a saucepan on the stovetop for 2–3 minutes over medium-low heat, just until butter is melted. Stir in adobo sauce, lime juice, cayenne pepper, and salt. Allow to cool slightly.

2. Rub ½ the adobo-and-margarine sauce over the corn on the cob, then grill for 6–8 minutes, rubbing again with the remaining mixture just before serving.

Yukon Gold Potatoes with Oregano

Serves 4

4 Yukon Gold potatoes, scrubbed

¼ cup olive oil

4 teaspoons dried oregano

Salt and fresh ground pepper to taste

Yukon Gold potatoes stand up to frying and grilling and are readily available year-round. The generous amount of oil in this recipe helps the potatoes come out golden and crisped. Reduce it if you'd like, but it won't be quite the same.

1. Cut the potatoes in quarters lengthwise and place on a piece of aluminum foil. Drizzle with olive oil and sprinkle with oregano, salt, and pepper.

2. Place on grill over medium heat, lid closed, and let bake for 20 minutes; check often. They're done when the outside is brown and crunchy and the inside is soft.

Grill-Roasted Sunchokes

Serves 4

2 pounds unpeeled sunchokes, chopped into 1" chunks
1 teaspoon olive oil
1½ teaspoons soy sauce
2 cloves garlic, minced
¼ cup green onions, coarsely chopped

Wrapping sunchokes in foil seals in all the great juices, and the touch of soy sauce balances their natural sweetness.

1. Place ½ of chopped sunchokes in the center of a large sheet of aluminum foil. Repeat with remaining sunchokes.

2. Drizzle each foil packet with olive oil and soy sauce, and add ½ of garlic and green onions to each.

3. Wrap up foil packets and seal tightly. Place on the grill over medium-low heat for 15 minutes, turning once, until soft. Open carefully.

Cooking with Sunchokes

Also called Jerusalem artichokes, sunchokes are ugly little tubers that look a bit like large knobs of ginger. When sealed in foil and grilled, as in this recipe, they taste something like a cross between a creamy sweet potato and a salty macadamia nut. They can be roasted in foil or placed directly on the grates, just like potatoes. Try them in place of potatoes in Rosemary Grilled Potatoes (see Chapter 4) or Maple Dijon Sweet Potatoes (see Chapter 4).

Basil Buttered Corn

Serves 4

3 tablespoons vegan margarine

2 tablespoons fresh basil, minced

½ cup green onions, chopped

Salt and pepper to taste

4 ears fresh sweet corn, husks removed

Corn begins to lose its sweetness the moment it is picked, so the shorter the time from garden to grill, the sweeter your corn will be. Extreme corn fanciers have been known to build a fire right next to their corn stalks so that the time to the grill is minimal.

1. Melt margarine in a saucepan over low heat. Add basil, onions, salt, and pepper, and mix. Drizzle mixture over corn.

2. Wrap each ear of corn individually in foil. Place on hot grill for about 20 minutes, turning once.

Tzatziki Stuffed Potatoes

Serves 4

⅔ cup plain yogurt

1 teaspoon lemon juice

1 teaspoon olive oil

½ medium cucumber, grated

½ teaspoon garlic powder

Dash salt and pepper

4 medium potatoes

2 tablespoons chopped fresh chives or green onions

For an authentic tzatziki flavor, use natural Greek yogurt. Choose vegan yogurt to make these grill-baked potatoes vegan.

1. Combine yogurt with lemon juice and olive oil until smooth. Add cucumber, garlic powder, salt, and pepper. Set tzatziki aside.

2. Wrap potatoes in foil and grill for 35–40 minutes, turning occasionally.

3. Slice cooked potatoes in half and scoop out enough of the center to make a shell, reserving cooked potato.

4. Combine cooked potato flesh with ½ of the tzatziki mixture. Return potatoes to grill, and cook until just warmed through. Garnish with a dollop of extra tzatziki and chopped fresh chives or green onions.

Chapter 5

Grilled Vegetables, Squash, and Sides

Garlicky Grilled Cauliflower

Serves 4

2 tablespoons vegan margarine, softened

1 medium-large cauliflower, whole

¾ teaspoon garlic salt

½ teaspoon onion powder

1 tablespoon nutritional yeast, or to taste

Add a bit of color to this cauliflower with a dash of nutmeg, cayenne, or paprika—but certainly not all three!

1. Spread margarine evenly over cauliflower and sprinkle with garlic salt and onion powder.

2. Wrap whole cauliflower tightly in aluminum foil and place on grill over medium heat. Allow to cook for 40–50 minutes, or until soft.

3. Remove from grill, carefully open foil, and sprinkle with nutritional yeast and serve hot.

Tequila Lime Skewers

Serves 2

¼ cup good quality tequila

3 tablespoons olive oil

3 tablespoons lime juice

1 teaspoon brown sugar

3 cloves garlic, minced

¼ teaspoon salt

12 button mushrooms

½ pineapple, chopped into 1" chunks

1 green bell pepper, chopped into chunks

You simply must play some Jimmy Buffet while whisking up these Margaritaville-inspired tropical skewers. Best enjoyed at sunset on the beach of an exotic tropical locale. Or in your backyard with a beer. Either way. If you want to vary the ingredients, try adding mango, tofu, or chili peppers.

1. Whisk together the tequila, olive oil, lime juice, brown sugar, garlic, and salt. Marinate the mushrooms, pineapple, and bell pepper for at least an hour, turning occasionally to coat well.

2. Place ingredients on skewers and grill over medium-high heat for 5–6 minutes on each side, brushing frequently with the extra sauce.

3. Drizzle with just a touch of the extra marinade—not too much—it's potent stuff!

Getting a Reaction

Marinades usually have some kind of acid in the mix, such as wine or citrus fruit juices. These acids will react with most metals, and that reaction will give your food a bad taste. It's best to marinate in glass or porcelain-covered metal.

Lemon Asparagus

Serves 3

1 pound fresh asparagus, trimmed

2 tablespoons olive oil

1 tablespoon lemon juice

Salt and pepper to taste (sea salt or kosher salt is best)

1½ tablespoons toasted pine nuts (optional)

Fresh asparagus comes alive on the grill with just a dash of salt, a drizzle of oil, and a squeeze of lemon. The pine nuts just class it up a bit for company.

1. Drizzle asparagus with olive oil and lemon juice and season with salt and pepper.

2. If needed, skewer the asparagus across the bottom and again halfway up.

3. Over medium to low heat, grill for about 8–10 minutes per side, depending on the heat of the grill and the thickness of the spears, being careful not to overcook.

4. Remove from grill and sprinkle pine nuts on top.

Jalapeño Mango Skewers

Serves 2

1 mango, chopped into 1" chunks

4 jalapeño peppers, chopped

1 medium onion, chopped

1 red bell pepper, chopped

Oil for brushing

Sea salt or kosher salt and fresh ground pepper to taste

Juice from 1 lime

2 tablespoons chopped fresh cilantro (optional)

To make a grilled mango salsa, finely chop all the ingredients together with a squeeze or two of lime juice.

1. Alternate mango, jalapeño peppers, onion, and bell pepper on skewers. Brush well with oil and season generously with salt and pepper.

2. Place skewers on the grill over medium heat for 4–5 minutes on each side, until veggies are cooked and mangoes are marked.

3. Drizzle with fresh lime juice and fresh chopped cilantro (if desired) just before serving.

Maple Chipotle Squash Wedges

Serves 3

1 unpeeled acorn squash, chopped into thick wedges
¼ cup vegan margarine, melted, divided
3 tablespoons maple syrup
1–2 teaspoons minced chipotle in adobo
1 teaspoon adobo sauce
¼ teaspoon salt

Pumpkin will work well in this recipe, too. Lightly score the squash to give it more surface area to hold all the sweet maple glaze.

1. Brush squash generously with 2 tablespoons of melted margarine.

2. Combine remaining margarine with maple syrup, chipotle, adobo sauce, and salt.

3. Place squash directly on the grill for about 10–12 minutes, then baste with maple sauce. Grill 5 more minutes, turn, baste again, and grill 1 or 2 more minutes, until soft.

Working with Winter Squashes

Squash takes a bit of effort to prepare, and you may be tempted to just skip ahead in search of easier recipes. But wait! A few tips and tricks can make working with squash less of a chore. First, to make the squash easier to chop, pierce it a few times with a knife, then stick it in the microwave for a minute or two, just to soften it up a bit. Using a sharp top-quality knife makes the chopping job much easier. To reduce the grilling time, microwave the squash whole for 5–7 minutes.

Grilled Vegetable Antipasto

Serves 8

1 medium eggplant, cut in wedges, lightly salted

2 yellow squash, quartered lengthwise

2 zucchini, quartered lengthwise

4 plum tomatoes, halved lengthwise

½ cup plus 2 tablespoons olive oil, divided

Pinch of crushed red pepper (optional)

Salt and pepper, divided

8 portobello mushrooms, stems removed

2 heads radicchio, core intact, quartered

1 tablespoon balsamic vinegar

Pinch of sugar (optional)

2 shallots, finely chopped

4 sprigs fresh thyme, leaves picked and chopped

8 sprigs fresh parsley

This assortment of grilled vegetables can serve as a flavorful accompaniment to any summer menu.

1. In a large mixing bowl, toss eggplant, squash, zucchini, and tomatoes with 1 tablespoon olive oil, crushed red pepper (if desired), and a bit of salt and pepper. Brush 1 tablespoon olive oil on tops of mushrooms and radicchio and season well with salt and pepper.

2. Cook vegetables on the grill over medium heat, without turning, until they are slightly more than halfway done. Eggplant and mushrooms will take longest, while the radicchio will take only a few minutes. Cook the tomatoes skin-side down only. Turn the other vegetables to finish, then arrange on a serving platter.

3. Whisk together remaining ½ cup olive oil, vinegar, sugar, shallots, and thyme. Season with salt and pepper to taste, and drizzle over cooked vegetables while they're still warm. Marinate 20 minutes before serving. Garnish with fresh parsley sprigs.

Honey Gingered Brussels Sprouts

Serves 4

1 tablespoon sesame oil

1 tablespoon honey

1 teaspoon minced fresh ginger

1 tablespoon soy sauce

2 cloves garlic, minced

1 pound Brussels sprouts

The reason you hated Brussels sprouts as a kid was because they were overcooked and underflavored. Grilling them softens these little cabbages just enough, and the golden brown charring from the grill is wonderfully appetizing.

1. Whisk together the sesame oil, honey, ginger, soy sauce, and garlic and toss with Brussels sprouts to coat. Marinate for at least 20 minutes. Reserve marinade.

2. Place the Brussels sprouts whole on the grill, or skewer or use a grill pan as needed.

3. Baste Brussels sprouts with extra marinade, and grill for 5–6 minutes. Turn, baste again, and heat for another 5–6 minutes or until done.

4. Toss with any extra marinade just before serving.

Thai Basil Eggplant

Serves 4

2 tablespoons soy sauce
2 tablespoons brown sugar
1 tablespoon sesame oil
2 tablespoons chopped fresh basil
1 large eggplant, chopped

Slice the eggplant into wedges or strips for a side dish, or chop into thick rounds to serve as an entrée.

1. Whisk together the soy sauce, brown sugar, sesame oil, and basil. Marinate eggplant for at least 20 minutes, turning occasionally to coat well. Reserve marinade.

2. Grill eggplant for 10–15 minutes, turning once and basting occasionally with just a bit of the extra sauce.

Types of Basil

Sweet Italian basil may be the most common, but other varieties add a layer of enticing flavor to otherwise simple dishes. Lemon basil has a lighter green color and fresh citrusy scent. For a delightfully scorching flavor, look for spicy holy basil or Thai basil with a purplish stem and jagged leaf edge to use in this recipe.

Summer Squash Boats

Serves 4

4 medium zucchinis or yellow squashes

½ cup olive oil

½ cup onion, chopped

2 cloves Roasted Garlic (see Chapter 2), mashed

½ cup bread crumbs

2 sprigs fresh mint, chopped, or two teaspoons dried

1 teaspoon paprika

Salt and fresh ground pepper

¼ cup grated Parmesan cheese

If you like fried zucchini, you'll love this healthier grilled version topped with bread crumbs and Parmesan. Use nutritional yeast instead of the Parmesan to make it vegan.

1. Rinse the zucchinis and dry them with paper towels. Cut the top third off horizontally. Using a melon baller, scoop out the centers of the squashes, reserving the pulp.

2. Heat the olive oil and sauté the onion and reserved squash pulp until soft. Remove from heat and stir in the roasted garlic, bread crumbs, and mint, then add the paprika, salt, pepper, and Parmesan cheese.

3. Place the "boats" on a piece of foil and cook on a grill over medium-high heat for 20 minutes, or until browned. Add the squash mixture to the boats and serve.

Broccolini Romano

Serves 4

2 tablespoons lemon juice

2 tablespoons olive oil

¼ teaspoon sea salt or kosher salt

⅛ teaspoon fresh ground black pepper

1 pound broccolini

⅓ cup fresh grated Romano or Pecorino Romano cheese

Use regular broccoli if you can't find broccolini. For a vegan version, omit the cheese and finish it off with nutritional yeast or a vegan Parmesan cheese.

1. Whisk together lemon juice, olive oil, salt, and pepper to combine. Toss with broccolini, and allow to marinate for at least 20 minutes.

2. Place broccolini on a well-greased grill over low or indirect heat. Grill for 6–8 minutes on each side.

3. Transfer to a serving dish and immediately coat with Romano, gently tossing to combine and warm the cheese.

Cabbage Patch Packets

Serves 4

Vegetable oil or nonstick spray

1 head cabbage, quartered and cored

1 onion, chopped

¼ cup vegan margarine, divided

Salt and fresh ground pepper

Toss these cabbage and onion packets on the grill for your St. Paddy's Day cookout to help wash down all that green stout. Keep it a bit crisp to add to salads, or grill until softened to use as a side dish.

1. Oil 4 large squares of aluminum foil with vegetable oil. On each square, place ¼ of the cabbage, ¼ of the onion, and 1 tablespoon of the margarine.

2. Sprinkle with salt and pepper and fold edges of foil to seal. Grill over low heat for 25–30 minutes, or until the cabbage is done to your liking, turning occasionally to avoid burning.

Easiest Veggie Kebabs in the World

Serves 2 as an entrée or 4 as a side

16 cherry tomatoes

16 button mushrooms

1 cup any other veggies, chopped into 1" chunks (try zucchini, broccoli, or cauliflower florets)

⅓ cup store-bought Italian salad dressing (or any other bottled marinade)

Empty cupboards? Don't feel like running to the store? Grab whatever veggies you've got in your fridge and a bottle of salad dressing, pack up the beers and kids, and you're good to grill with this recipe.

1. Marinate veggies in salad dressing for at least 20 minutes, making sure they're all coated.

2. Arrange veggies on skewers, then grill for about 10 minutes, brushing lightly with extra dressing, turning once.

Marinating Tips

A wide shallow pan works for marinating most ingredients. Even better, pour your marinades into a large resealable plastic bag, then add your ingredients and seal well, pushing out as much air as possible from the bag (triple-check the seal to avoid a messy fridge!). Put it in the fridge, and just shake it gently or turn it over once in a while to make sure everything is coated evenly.

Grilled Pumpkin Wedges with Maple Butter

Serves 4

1 medium-small sugar pumpkin

¼ cup vegan margarine, softened

¼ cup maple syrup

¼ teaspoon sea salt

½ teaspoon cinnamon or nutmeg (optional)

Leaving the inedible skin on when cooking squash gives it a rustic homey appearance. If it bothers you, though, remove it with a vegetable peeler.

1. Chop pumpkin in half and remove seeds and stringy bits. Chop pumpkin into thick wedges.

2. Whisk together the softened margarine, maple syrup, salt, and cinnamon. Brush well over both sides of each pumpkin wedge.

3. Grill over low or indirect heat for 20–25 minutes, turning once, until soft. Drizzle with any remaining sauce just before serving.

Miso-Glazed Eggplant

Serves 6

2 tablespoons miso

2 teaspoons fresh minced ginger

2 teaspoons sugar

2 teaspoons sesame oil

1 tablespoon olive oil

3 cloves garlic, minced

3 tablespoons water

2 medium-large eggplants, sliced into rounds about ¾" thick

Olive oil for brushing

¼ cup chopped scallions or fresh cilantro, for garnish (optional)

Miso is a flavorful addition to a variety of dishes. If you find it a bit overpowering, try thinning out the glaze with a few extra spoonfuls of liquid, and using a scant amount of the required miso.

1. Whisk together miso, ginger, sugar, sesame oil, olive oil, garlic, and water.

2. Lightly brush eggplant rounds with olive oil on one side. Spread a layer of the miso paste on the other.

3. Place on grill over medium-low heat, miso-side up. Grill for 4–5 minutes, then turn. Spread another layer of the miso paste on top of the eggplant and heat for another 4–5 minutes, or until eggplant has cooked. Garnish with chopped scallions or fresh cilantro.

Lemon Oregano Summer Squash Skewers

Serves 3

3 tablespoons olive oil

1 tablespoon lemon juice

1 teaspoon oregano

½ teaspoon lemon pepper

2 zucchinis, chopped into 1"-thick chunks

2 yellow summer squashes, chopped into 1"-thick slices

For extra flavor, add in some onions, button mushrooms, or cherry tomatoes.

1. Whisk together olive oil, lemon juice, oregano, and lemon pepper until well combined. Marinate veggies in mixture for at least 20 minutes.

2. Place marinated veggies on skewers and grill for 8–10 minutes, turning once. Drizzle with a bit of extra sauce just before serving, if desired.

Honey Mustard Beets

Serves 4

2 tablespoons honey or agave nectar

1½ tablespoons Dijon mustard

2 teaspoons lemon juice

1 tablespoon olive oil

Salt and pepper to taste

4 medium beets, peeled and chopped into 1" chunks

When grilling beets, the smaller the dice, the more surface area and flavor—and the shorter the cooking time.

1. Whisk together the honey, Dijon, lemon juice, olive oil, salt, and pepper.

2. Place beets on foil, drizzle with all of the sauce, then wrap tightly and grill 15–20 minutes, turning once.

Grilling Beets

Like many vegetables, beets work well directly on the grill with just a coating of oil, salt, and pepper. Wrapping them in foil, as in this recipe, locks in both moisture and flavor, as they do tend to dry out a bit when placed directly on the grill.

Grilled Onions with Balsamic Glaze

Serves 4

4 large sweet onions
2 tablespoons olive oil
Kosher salt and fresh ground black pepper
1 cup balsamic vinegar

The key to perfect, sweet grilled onions is slow, even cooking over just a whisper of a low flame. These grilled onions make great veggie burger toppers.

1. Trim off the ends of the onions, about ½" from the root and sprout ends. Halve the onions widthwise. Brush with olive oil and sprinkle with salt and pepper to taste.

2. In a saucepan over medium heat, simmer the balsamic vinegar until it has reduced by half and cooked down to a thick syrup.

3. Place the onion slices on the grill over low heat and cook slowly without moving them, for about 15 minutes, until dark grill marks appear. Turn once, using both tongs and a spatula to keep the rings together. Grill until the second side is well marked and juices begin to pool on the top, another 10 minutes.

4. Brush with balsamic syrup 5 minutes before removing from the grill. Drizzle with remaining syrup and serve.

Curried Squash Kebabs

Serves 4

1 medium butternut squash
2 tablespoons vegan margarine, softened
2 teaspoons curry powder
½ teaspoon cumin
¼ teaspoon cayenne pepper, or to taste
Sea salt or kosher salt to taste

If you like curried squash soup, you'll like this similarly flavored grilled recipe.

1. Pierce butternut squash several times with a knife, and place in the microwave for 1–2 minutes to soften it up. Cool. Peel and chop into 1" chunks.

2. Rub squash chunks with margarine, then skewer. Sprinkle all over with curry powder, cumin, cayenne pepper, and a bit of salt.

3. Place on the grill over medium heat for 12–15 minutes, turning once or twice, until soft.

Veggie "Stir-Fry" Packets

Serves 4 as a side dish or 3 as an entrée

1 cup broccoli florets, chopped small

1 medium carrot, sliced thin

½ cup snow peas

½ cup sliced mushrooms

3 cloves garlic, minced

1 tablespoon soy sauce

1 tablespoon olive oil

2 teaspoons sesame oil

1 tablespoon rice vinegar

1 teaspoon fresh minced ginger

Pair these "hobo packets" with rice or noodles for a full meal, perhaps alongside an Asian-inspired grilled tofu such as Hoisin-Glazed Tofu (see Chapter 7). Vary the vegetables to taste: try red bell pepper, yellow squash, or red onions.

1. Combine broccoli, carrot, snow peas, mushrooms, and garlic in a large bowl.

2. In a separate small bowl, whisk together remaining ingredients. Toss with veggies to coat well.

3. Divide veggie mixture into quarters, and wrap each tightly in foil, making sure to include plenty of liquid in each packet so that none is left over.

4. Grill for 10–12 minutes, turning once.

Roasted Peppers on the Grill

Makes 2 roasted red peppers

2 large red or yellow bell peppers, halved and seeded
2 teaspoons olive oil

Use your grill-roasted peppers on top of veggie burgers, in recipes, or as a condiment to any grilled meal.

1. Brush the skins of the peppers with olive oil. Grill the peppers skin-side down until charred. Do not turn them.

2. Place the peppers in a plastic or paper bag to cool. As they cool, their skins loosen and are easily removed.

Roasting Indoors

Oven roasted red peppers don't have the smoky flavor that grilled ones do, but they're still excellent. To make these indoors, fire up your oven to 450°F (or use the broiler setting) and drizzle a few whole peppers with olive oil. Bake for 30 minutes, turning over once. Direct heat will also work indoors, if you have a gas stove. Hold the peppers with tongs over the flame until lightly charred. Let your peppers cool, then remove the skins.

Herbed Leeks with Lemon

Serves 4

4 leeks, cleaned, split lengthwise

Salted water for boiling

3 tablespoons olive oil, divided

Kosher salt and fresh ground black pepper

1 teaspoon Dijon mustard

2 teaspoons fresh-squeezed lemon juice

1 tablespoon freshly chopped tarragon, chervil, chives, or Italian parsley

Leeks achieve a tender, silky texture and mild sweetness on the grill when they've been steamed or blanched in boiling water before they hit the barbecue. Always leave the root core attached to hold cooking leeks together.

1. Steam or blanch the leeks in boiling salted water for 5 minutes. Rinse in ice-cold water and drain well.

2. Brush leeks with 2 teaspoons olive oil, then season with salt and pepper.

3. Grill on both sides until dark-brown grill marks appear. Transfer to a platter.

4. Whisk together the Dijon mustard and lemon juice. Gradually whisk in the remaining olive oil and season the dressing with salt and pepper. Drizzle this dressing over the grilled leeks.

5. Sprinkle with chopped tarragon or other fresh herbs and serve hot.

Buttered Snow Peas

Serves 4

2 cups snow peas or sugar snap peas	*Munch these little peas as is (yes, they're that good) or add to a salad.*
1 teaspoon soy sauce	
2 tablespoons vegan margarine, melted	
Sea salt to taste	

2 cups snow peas or sugar snap peas

1 teaspoon soy sauce

2 tablespoons vegan margarine, melted

Sea salt to taste

Munch these little peas as is (yes, they're that good) or add to a salad.

1. Place snow peas on a large sheet of foil and drizzle with soy sauce and melted margarine. Wrap tightly, leaving extra space inside the packet for steam to circulate.

2. Place on the grill for 8–10 minutes, turning once. Open foil packets carefully and sprinkle with sea salt to taste.

French-Style Green Beans

Serves 4

1 pound string beans

1 quart water with 1 teaspoon salt added

¼ cup olive oil

6 fresh basil leaves, coarsely chopped, or 1 tablespoon dried basil

4 cloves garlic, minced

Salt and fresh ground pepper to taste

Green beans can be placed directly on the grill, or use a vegetable grill basket or a barbecue sheet cover to keep them from falling through the grates.

1. Rinse the beans and trim off the ends. Bring the salted water to a boil and parboil the beans for about 5 minutes. Shock the beans in icy cold water to keep them green. Drain and place on paper towels to dry.

2. Combine the remaining ingredients. Brush beans with olive oil mixture, then place on the grill over medium heat. Grill until lightly browned but not burned, about 10–15 minutes.

Sweet Worcestershire Grilled Onions

Serves 4 as a side dish or 8 as a condiment

2 large Vidalia or Bermuda onions

Salt and fresh ground pepper to taste

1 tablespoon cider vinegar

½ cup (1 stick) butter or margarine

1 tablespoon honey

1 tablespoon spicy brown mustard

1 teaspoon vegetarian Worcestershire sauce

Substitute agave nectar or a bit of sugar for the honey and use a nondairy margarine if you're cooking for vegans.

1. Remove the skins and ends from the onions and cut them crosswise in thick wedges. Sprinkle lightly with salt and pepper.

2. Combine the remaining ingredients in a small saucepan and warm until the butter melts.

3. Brush onions with the butter mixture and place on grill over medium heat. Grill for 3 minutes, turn, and grill 3 more minutes. Onions should be golden brown, but not burned.

Broccoli with Lemon Dill Sauce

Serves 6

2 tablespoons butter or margarine
2 tablespoons flour
1 teaspoon lemon zest
½ teaspoon fresh dill, minced
¼ teaspoon salt
¼ teaspoon paprika
1 cup milk or soy milk
1 head of broccoli, cut into chunks

Make the sauce while the broccoli is grilling if you can; otherwise, keep it warming on the stove.

1. Melt butter in a saucepan over low heat. Add flour, lemon zest, dill, salt, and paprika. Slowly whisk in milk or soymilk, stirring until thickened.

2. Place broccoli on a well-greased grill over low heat. Grill until soft, turning once, about 12–15 minutes. Transfer broccoli to a serving platter and cover with sauce to serve.

Raisin-Stuffed Acorn Squash

Serves 6

3 acorn squash

1 tablespoon vegetable oil

¼ cup raisins

¼ cup brown sugar, packed

2 tablespoons vegan margarine

Eat it with a spoon right out of the shell, or slice it into individual wedges so the kids can munch it like watermelon.

1. Cut squash in half and remove seeds. Place each half cut-side up on a sheet of aluminum foil. Brush cut sides with oil and sprinkle with raisins. Fold edges of foil to seal.

2. Grill squash over medium heat for 45 minutes, or until tender.

3. Carefully unwrap squash and sprinkle with brown sugar. Dot with margarine, rewrap, and grill for another 5 minutes.

Zucchini Slices with Italian Parsley

Serves 4

1 pound zucchini, cut lengthwise into ¼" slices

2 tablespoons olive oil, divided

⅜ teaspoon salt, divided

⅛ teaspoon black pepper

¼ teaspoon red wine vinegar

1 clove garlic, minced

1 tablespoon chopped Italian (flat-leaf) parsley

Zucchini works well on the grill, no matter what you do to it. This simple recipe pairs zucchini with Italian parsley in a red wine vinaigrette.

1. Toss zucchini with 1 tablespoon olive oil, ¼ teaspoon salt, and pepper in a bowl.

2. Grill the zucchini, turning once, until tender and golden, about 5 minutes on each side.

3. Combine remaining olive oil, remaining salt, red wine vinegar, garlic, and parsley in the same bowl and return the grilled zucchini to the bowl. Toss gently. Place zucchini on serving platter and sprinkle with extra olive oil, salt, and pepper to taste.

Chapter 6

Sandwiches and Burgers

Mozzarella Basil Panini

Serves 4

8 slices bread, any kind will do

Olive oil for brushing

1 6-ounce ball mozzarella cheese, sliced ½" thick

1 large tomato, sliced thick

8–12 fresh basil leaves

Salt and pepper to taste

A classically simple sandwich inspired by an Italian insalata caprese—tomatoes, mozzarella, basil, done.

1. Brush bread well with olive oil on one side. Pile mozzarella slices, tomato slices, and fresh basil on 4 slices of bread, sprinkle lightly with salt and pepper. Top each with another slice of bread to make a sandwich.

2. Grill 5–6 minutes over low heat, or just until bread is lightly toasted.

Grilled Falafel Patties

Serves 4

1 15-ounce can chickpeas, drained
2 slices whole-wheat bread
1 tablespoon lemon juice
3 cloves garlic, minced
1 teaspoon cumin
¼ teaspoon salt
¼ cup green onions, chopped
⅓ cup fresh parsley, chopped
2 tablespoons fresh cilantro or mint, chopped

Serve stuffed in a warmed pita with tzatziki or tahini sauce and fresh lemon wedges for color.

1. Process chickpeas, bread, lemon juice, garlic, cumin, and salt in a food processor until almost smooth. Add green onions, parsley, and cilantro. Pulse until herbs are finely chopped and combined.

2. Shape mixture into patties. Brush with olive oil on both sides. Place on grill over medium-low heat for 6–8 minutes on each side.

Portobello Patties with Pesto Mayonnaise

Serves 4

½ cup mayonnaise

3 tablespoons pesto

1 teaspoon lemon juice

½ teaspoon garlic salt

3 tablespoons olive oil

3 cloves garlic, minced

2 tablespoons balsamic vinegar

1 tablespoon soy sauce

4 portobellos, stems removed

It doesn't get easier than this. Some people prefer their portobellos with the stringy bits scraped off. I say, the more mushroom, the merrier—leave it on! For the wine, meaty portobellos work well with an equally "meaty" red wine; try a Pinot noir or a French Syrah.

1. Whisk together mayonnaise, pesto, lemon juice, and garlic salt. Set aside.

2. In a separate small bowl, whisk together the olive oil, minced garlic, vinegar, and soy sauce. Transfer to a shallow container or resealable plastic bag and add mushrooms. Allow to marinate for at least 30 minutes.

3. Grill over low heat for 3 minutes, turn, and grill for 3–4 more minutes. Give larger mushrooms an extra minute or two.

Cleaning a Portobello Mushroom

As with any mushroom variety, portobellos do not need rinsing, simply a thorough wipe-off with a moist paper towel. Then carefully twist off the mushroom's stem. Removing the black gills under the cap is optional. To do this, use a spoon and gently scrape them away. The gills impart a dark color to any surrounding liquids.

The "Reubenesque"

Serves 4

2 sweet onions, chopped thin

2 teaspoons olive oil

1 tablespoon vegan margarine

¼ teaspoon salt

½ teaspoon brown sugar (optional)

¼ cup barbecue sauce

3 tablespoons vinegar

2 tablespoons whole-grain or Dijon mustard

4 portobello mushroom caps

8 slices bread

¼ cup vegan Thousand Island dressing

If you don't care for rye bread, try this full-bodied and full-flavored Rubenesque Reuben on sourdough or French bread. A Reuben usually requires sauerkraut, but this version uses caramelized onions instead.

1. In a saucepan over low heat, cook onions with olive oil, margarine, salt, and brown sugar (if desired). Allow onions to cook down for at least 30 minutes, until well caramelized. Scrape pan frequently. Add a touch of water to deglaze the pan, if you need to.

2. Whisk together the barbecue sauce, vinegar, and mustard, then transfer to a shallow pan or resealable plastic bag. Add the mushrooms and marinate in the sauce for at least 30 minutes.

3. Grill mushrooms for 3–4 minutes on each side, over medium heat until soft.

4. To assemble sandwich, place grilled mushrooms on bread and top with caramelized onions and Thousand Island dressing. Return to grill for 1–2 minutes, until bread is lightly toasted.

Saucy Cheeseburger Sauce

Makes 1½ cups

2 tablespoons unsalted butter

2 tablespoons flour

1 shallot, minced

1 cup warm milk

Pinch ground nutmeg

4 ounces sharp Cheddar cheese

Fresh ground black pepper to taste

What's better than a veggie burger topped with this old-fashioned cheese sauce and some Sweet Worcestershire Grilled Onions (see Chapter 5)? And pickles. Lots of pickles.

1. Make a roux by melting the butter over low heat and stirring in the flour and shallot. Cook, stirring, for 3 minutes.

2. Add the milk and nutmeg, stirring until thickened. Stir in the cheese and turn off the stove. Add pepper to taste. Top veggie burgers with sauce.

Chewy TVP Burgers

Serves 4

2/3 cup TVP crumbles

2/3 cup hot water

1/2 vegetarian beef-flavored bouillon cube (optional)

Egg replacer for 2 eggs

1/2 onion, minced

2 tablespoons barbecue sauce

1/2 teaspoon garlic powder

3/4 teaspoon paprika

1/4 teaspoon chili powder

1/2 teaspoon salt

1/2 cup bread crumbs

2/3–3/4 cup flour

Olive oil for brushing

These veggie burgers are strictly chewy and meaty; no carrots allowed.

1. Place TVP in a medium bowl. Dissolve bouillon cube (if using) in the hot water and pour the water over TVP to reconstitute. Allow to sit for 6–7 minutes. Gently press to remove any excess moisture.

2. In a large bowl, combine the TVP, egg replacer, onion, barbecue sauce, and seasonings until mixed.

3. Add bread crumbs and combine, then add flour, a few tablespoons at a time, mixing to combine until mixture is sticky and thick. You may need a little more or less than 2/3 cup.

4. With lightly floured hands, shape mixture into patties 1½–2" thick. Place on a very well-greased grill over low heat for 3–4 minutes on each side.

TVP: Cheap, Chewy, and Meaty

TVP (textured vegetable protein) is inexpensive and has such a meaty texture that many budget-conscious nonvegetarian cooks use it to stretch their dollar, adding it to homemade burgers and meat loaves. For the best deal, buy it in bulk. TVP is usually found in small crumbles, which is what you want for this recipe, but it also comes in strips or chunks. Some health-food stores stock preflavored TVP, which comes in mock chicken, beef, and pork flavors—all vegetarian, of course.

Grilled Swiss Cheese with Apples

Serves 2

4 slices sourdough bread, thinly sliced

Olive oil or butter for brushing

4 slices vegetarian bacon substitute, cooked

1 apple, thinly sliced

⅓ cup Swiss cheese, grated

Swiss cheese goes well with sourdough bread, but feel free to experiment. Rye or olive bread might be interesting. If you're not a fan of vegetarian bacon, add a sprinkle of dried cranberries for an unexpected sweet bite.

1. Brush bread with olive oil or butter on one side. Place vegetarian bacon and apple slices on un-oiled side of bread, cover with grated Swiss cheese, and top with another slice of bread.

2. Place on grill for 1–2 minutes over low heat until cheese has melted. Allow to cool slightly before serving.

The Chocolate Elvis

Serves 4

8 slices bread

⅓ cup almond butter

2 bananas, sliced

¼ cup vegan chocolate chips

Olive oil or softened vegan margarine for brushing

If you're worried that this recipe isn't quite true to the King, you should know that almond butter fares better on the grill than peanut butter. Elvis would still likely approve.

1. Spread each slice of bread with a quarter of the almond butter and top each with ½ of a banana and 1 table-spoon chocolate chips. Top each off with another slice of bread, to make a sandwich.

2. Brush each side of sandwich with olive oil and grill for 4–6 minutes over low heat, turning once.

Mushroom Cheese Patties

Serves 4

2½ cups mushrooms, any kind, finely chopped

⅓ cup onion, diced

3 cloves garlic, minced

2 tablespoons olive oil, divided

½ cup oats

⅔ cup seasoned bread crumbs (toasted is best)

⅓ cup mozzarella or Swiss cheese, grated

2 teaspoons steak sauce

1 teaspoon seasoned salt (or salt and pepper to taste)

The best veggie burgers are those that have a solid sense of self—they aren't trying to be something they're not, they're just fantastic in their own right. These patties don't taste much like a traditional burger—they're better than beef. Promise.

1. Sauté mushrooms, onions, and garlic in 1 tablespoon olive oil until just soft, then combine with remaining ingredients.

2. Shape mixture into 4 large patties, then place on the grill over medium-low heat for 3–4 minutes on each side.

Raspberry Mascarpone on Brioche

Serves 1

2 thick slices brioche or other sweet bread

Olive oil for brushing

2 tablespoons raspberry jam

2 tablespoons mascarpone cheese

2 tablespoons chocolate chips

Unlike The Chocolate Elvis (see Chapter 6), or the Double Chocolate Diet Disaster Sandwich (see Chapter 10), this is a sandwich you don't have to feel the least bit guilty about eating. Nor do you have to hide it from your friends—it's meant for adults!

1. Brush bread well with olive oil. Spread one slice with jam, the other with mascarpone, then sprinkle with chocolate chips.

2. Place over low heat on grill, just until lightly toasted, a couple of minutes on each side.

Turn This Recipe into a Decadent Dessert

Slice this sandwich into finger-food sizes and serve with vanilla or chocolate chip ice cream.

Eggplant and Hummus Panini

Serves 4

2 tablespoons olive oil

2 teaspoons balsamic vinegar

¼ teaspoon basil

¼ teaspoon oregano

1 small eggplant, sliced ¾" thick

1 small zucchini or yellow squash, sliced ¾" thick

1 recipe Roasted Peppers on the Grill, sliced (see Chapter 5)

½ cup hummus

8 slices bread

Made with hummus instead of cheese, this eggplant-and-roasted-red-pepper panini is as healthy as it is tasty. Try it with a flavored hummus.

1. Whisk together olive oil, balsamic vinegar, basil, and oregano, then brush eggplant and squash well on both sides. Grill until very soft, basting with extra sauce.

2. Layer grilled vegetables on bread along with a layer of hummus and some roasted red pepper slices. Assemble the sandwich, brush with extra olive oil, and grill just until bread is toasted and sandwich is warmed through.

Super Easy Black Bean Burgers

Serves 4

1 15-ounce can black beans, drained
3 tablespoons minced onions
1 teaspoon salt
1½ teaspoons garlic powder
2 teaspoons parsley
1 teaspoon chili powder
⅔ cup flour
Olive oil for brushing

This is the easiest recipe for black bean burgers you'll ever find. Mash some beans, add a bit of flavor and a bit of flour to hold it all together, and you've got yourself a burger.

1. Process the black beans in a blender or food processor until halfway mashed, or mash with a fork. Add minced onions, salt, garlic powder, parsley, and chili powder and mash to combine.

2. Add flour a bit at time, again mashing together to combine. You may need a little bit more or less than ⅔ cup. Beans should stick together completely.

3. Form into patties and brush with oil on both sides. Place on a well-greased grill over low heat for 3–4 minutes per side.

Veggie Burger Tips

Although this recipe is foolproof, if you have trouble with your homemade veggie burgers crumbling, try adding egg replacer to bind the ingredients, then chill the mixture before forming it into patties. Do your veggie burgers dry out a bit on the grill? Grill them over a higher temperature. Still have a problem? Just smother dry patties with extra ketchup!

Tofu and Pesto Panini on Ciabatta

Serves 4

Ciabatta bread or rolls for 4 sandwiches, sliced in half

Olive oil for brushing

¼ cup prepared pesto

¼ cup olive tapenade

4 slices Easy Herb-Marinated Tofu (see Chapter 7), or another grilled tofu

½ cup chopped sun-dried tomatoes (oil-packed or rehydrated)

1 cup baby spinach, loosely packed (optional)

¼ cup mayonnaise

Use up your leftover grilled tofu in this flavorful panini.

1. Brush each slice of bread with olive oil on one side. On four of the bread slices, spread a layer of pesto, then a layer of tapenade. Add tofu slices, sun-dried tomatoes, and spinach, if using. On the other four bread slices, spread a layer of mayonnaise, then place on top of the tofu-layered slices to make sandwiches.

2. Place on grill over low heat just until bread is well-toasted.

Brown Rice and Bean Burgers

Serves 6

3 tablespoons olive oil
1 small yellow onion, chopped small
1 small green bell pepper, chopped small
2 cloves garlic, minced
1½ cups cooked brown rice
2 cups cooked black beans
2 tablespoons tomato paste
1 teaspoon ground cumin
½ cup Italian (flat-leaf) parsley, chopped fine
Salt and pepper to taste

This versatile recipe can be seasoned according to your own preferences. Try adding onion powder and paprika, or perhaps oregano and poultry seasoning just for fun. Why not? Serve with salsa.

1. Heat the olive oil in a sauté pan over medium. Add the onion, green bell pepper, and garlic and sauté over low flame until soft, about 10 minutes.

2. Place the cooked peppers and onions in a bowl. Add rice, beans, tomato paste, cumin, parsley, salt, and pepper. Mash the mixture with a potato masher.

3. Form into patties and place over medium heat on the grill for 4 minutes. Turn and grill 4 more minutes until nice and hot.

Italian Kalamata and Four-Cheese Panini

Serves 4

¼ cup olive oil

1 teaspoon thyme

2 cloves garlic, minced

20 kalamata or Sicilian olives, pitted and chopped

1 teaspoon fresh ground black pepper, or to taste

8 slices Tuscan bread, sliced thin, about ¼" thick

8 slices provolone cheese

8 slices mozzarella cheese

4 recipes Roasted Peppers on the Grill (see Chapter 5)

8 slices tomato

½ cup Gorgonzola cheese, crumbled

½ cup Parmesan cheese, grated

These cheesy panini are kind of like little smooshed pizzas. Slice Italian country bread on the diagonal, or try it on ciabatta rolls. Jarred roasted red peppers work as well as homemade.

1. Mix the oil, thyme, garlic, olives, and black pepper, and brush the bread slices with the mixture.

2. On each piece of bread, layer a slice of provolone, a slice of mozzarella, a red pepper, and a tomato slice. On 4 of the pieces of bread, end with tomato, and on the other 4, end with red pepper. Sprinkle each piece of layered bread with the crumbled Gorgonzola and Parmesan cheeses. Close sandwiches so that pieces with tomato meet pieces with red pepper. Brush each sandwich with extra olive oil.

3. Place on grill over medium heat and grill until the cheeses are melted and bread is browned.

Panini for Starving Artists

You don't need a grill or a panini maker to press an excellent panini if you have two pans and a stovetop range. Here's how: Place the sandwiches in a heavy cast-iron skillet or stovetop grill pan. Lightly grease the underneath (yes, the bottom) of another pan and place on top of the sandwich. Weight the top pan down with a brick, a couple of heavy cans, or whatever weight you can find. Voilà!

Easy Peasy Portobello Patties

Serves 3

| 1 cup balsamic vinaigrette |
| 3 large portobello mushrooms |

It doesn't take much to make portobellos taste fantastic on the grill; nature has already done most of the work for you. A quick marinade in a store-bought or homemade balsamic vinaigrette dressing will work wonders, and even the heartiest of carnivores loves a good grilled mushroom, so make plenty to share and use them to fill up your burgers.

1. Marinate the mushrooms for 1–2 hours in the balsamic vinaigrette.

2. Grill over medium-low heat for 3 minutes, turn, and grill for 3–4 more minutes, heating 1–2 more minutes for larger mushrooms.

Chipotle Bean Burgers

Serves 4

1 15-ounce can black beans

¼ cup onion, minced

½ green bell pepper, minced

1 chipotle chili in adobo, minced

1 egg, beaten

1 tablespoon adobo sauce

½ cup bread crumbs

Oil for brushing

Smoky chipotle chili peppers add a Southwestern taste to these otherwise ordinary black bean burgers. Whisk together a bit of the extra adobo sauce with some mayonnaise to top it all off. These spicy burgers pair well with a sweet or tart beer, such as a fruited Belgian lambic.

1. Drain and rinse beans, then gently pat dry.

2. Smash beans, using a fork or potato masher, until mostly smooth. Add onion, bell pepper, and chili. Mix well.

3. Add in egg and adobo sauce, mixing to combine, then add bread crumbs. You may need to use a little bit more or less than ½ cup. Mixture should be thick and hold together.

4. Form mixture into 1"-thick patties. If mixture will not hold, chill for 30 minutes first, then form into patties. Brush with oil, then grill over medium-low heat for 3–4 minutes on each side.

Chapter 7

Tofu on the Grill

Mojito-Marinated Tofu

Serves 4

1 tablespoon soy sauce

¼ cup fresh mint, minced

1 tablespoon olive oil

¼ cup lime juice

1 teaspoon rum extract

3 tablespoons honey or agave nectar

1 16-ounce package firm or extra-firm tofu, well pressed, sliced

Inspired by the classic Cuban cocktail, the rum flavor comes from rum extract, rather than liquor, which technically makes this tofu dish virgin. The fresh and minty tofu is a flavor departure from the usual more savory grilled tofu recipes.

1. Whisk together all ingredients except tofu and transfer to a shallow pan or resealable plastic bag. Add tofu and allow to marinate for at least 1 hour.

2. Place marinated tofu on grill over medium heat for 5–6 minutes, turning once and basting once or twice. Drizzle with just a touch of the extra marinade or garnish with extra fresh mint.

Cumin-Rubbed Tofu

Serves 4

1 16-ounce package firm or extra-firm tofu, well-pressed, sliced

Olive oil for brushing

1 teaspoon cumin

½ teaspoon oregano

½ teaspoon garlic salt

½ teaspoon onion powder

¼ teaspoon paprika

Cumin, native to many global cuisines, including Mexican and Indian, lends a unique exotic flavor to any dish.

1. Brush tofu with olive oil on both sides.

2. In a small bowl, combine all of the spices, then gently rub over the tofu on both sides.

3. Place tofu on grill over medium heat for 5–6 minutes, turning once or as needed.

Hoisin-Glazed Tofu

Serves 4

2 tablespoons hoisin sauce
2 tablespoons sesame oil
1 teaspoon fresh minced ginger
1 tablespoon rice vinegar
1–2 tablespoons water
2 cloves garlic, minced
½ teaspoon crushed red pepper flakes (optional)
1 16-ounce package firm or extra-firm tofu, sliced

This recipe tames the strong taste of hoisin sauce by combining it with other flavors.

1. Whisk together all ingredients except tofu until combined. Marinate tofu in sauce mixture for at least 20 minutes, turning occasionally to make sure tofu is coated.

2. Place tofu over medium-high heat on the grill and brush with extra sauce. Grill for 5–6 minutes on each side, brushing occasionally with extra sauce.

Pressing Tofu

Tofu doesn't taste like much on its own, but it soaks up spices and marinades wonderfully. It's like a sponge: the drier it is, the more flavor it absorbs. Wrap firm tofu in a couple of layers of paper towels and place a can of beans or another light weight on top. After 10 minutes, flip the tofu over and let it sit weighted down for another 10 minutes. Pressing firm and extra-firm tofu allows it to absorb even more of whatever it marinates in.

Sticky Sweet Tofu

Serves 4

¼ cup barbecue sauce

3 tablespoons soy sauce

2 tablespoons brown sugar

1 tablespoon oil

1 tablespoon water

1 teaspoon hot sauce (optional)

1 16-ounce package firm or extra-firm tofu, sliced

Don't be fooled by the simplicity of this recipe—you'll be licking your fingers (and the spoon and the bowl) shamelessly. The marinade also makes a great dip to serve with the tofu.

1. Whisk together the barbecue sauce, soy sauce, brown sugar, oil, water, and hot sauce (if desired). Marinate tofu in mixture for at least 30 minutes—the longer the better.

2. Place tofu over medium-high heat on the grill and brush with extra sauce. Grill for 5–6 minutes on each side, brushing occasionally with extra sauce. Serve topped with any extra marinade.

Tuscan Wine-Marinated Tofu and Shallot Skewers

Serves 4

¼ cup red wine

2 cloves garlic, minced

2 tablespoons olive oil

1 tablespoon soy sauce

2 teaspoons Italian seasoning

¼ teaspoon red pepper flakes (optional)

1 16-ounce package firm or extra-firm tofu, pressed, then chopped into 1" cubes

16 button mushrooms

16 shallots

Chianti is native to Tuscany, so use it to add authenticity to this marinated tofu. Place fresh sprigs of thyme or rosemary right on the coals for a smoky herb flavor, and use bamboo skewers soaked in wine for an unforgettable experience. Perfetto!

1. Whisk together the red wine, garlic, olive oil, soy sauce, Italian seasoning, and red pepper flakes (if desired). In a shallow pan or resealable plastic bag, marinate the tofu, mushrooms, and shallots for at least 30 minutes, turning as needed to cover with marinade.

2. Thread tofu, mushrooms, and shallots on soaked skewers, alternating ingredients. Place over medium heat on the grill, turning occasionally, for 8–10 minutes, or until tofu has cooked and shallots are soft.

About Those Shallots

Shallots larger than about ¾" in diameter should be chopped in half for this recipe. If you can't find shallots, halved pearl onions would be a reasonable substitute, though they don't have the same depth of flavor as shallots. While you're at it, why not make an extra skewer of just shallots, then mash them and use as a crostini topper?

Dengaku Miso Tofu

Serves 4

¼ cup miso

3 tablespoons water

2 tablespoons brown sugar

2 teaspoons sesame oil

2 tablespoons rice vinegar

1 16-ounce package firm or extra-firm tofu, well-pressed and cut into thin slabs

Olive oil for brushing

Dengaku, literally "on stilts" in Japanese, are tofu slabs grilled on two skewers—tofu on stilts! This sweet and salty miso mixture caramelizes into a beautiful glaze when placed over the hot fire.

1. Over low heat, whisk together the miso and water in a saucepan, until smooth and creamy, then stir in brown sugar, oil, and rice vinegar until mixed.

2. Brush tofu with olive oil, then place on the grill over medium heat for 4–5 minutes on each side, until lightly browned.

3. Baste tofu with miso sauce, and return to the grill over high heat for 1–2 minutes on each side, until glaze is caramelized and browned.

Easy Herb-Marinated Tofu

Serves 4

3 tablespoons lemon juice

2 tablespoons olive oil

3 cloves garlic, minced

1 tablespoon chopped fresh basil

1 teaspoon chopped fresh rosemary

1 16-ounce package firm or extra-firm tofu, sliced

Salt and fresh ground pepper to taste

A simple grilled tofu recipe or two is essential for every vegetarian backyard chef. After you try it once, you won't even have to think about it—lemon juice, olive oil, garlic, herbs, and voilà!

1. Whisk together the lemon juice, olive oil, and garlic until emulsified, then add in basil and rosemary. Marinate tofu for at least 20 minutes, up to overnight—the longer the better.

2. Remove the tofu from the marinade and season with salt and pepper to taste. Place on a well-greased grill over medium heat for 5–6 minutes on each side.

Leftover Grilled Tofu

The flavors in this herbed tofu are fresh, familiar, and tasty, and go with just about anything. Add these tofu pieces to a green salad or pasta salad; try them on top of grilled pizza or on a whole-grain bun. Make a double batch and add leftover pieces to stir-fries, sandwich wraps, or lunchboxes.

Spaghetti-Flavored Tofu

Serves 4

¼ cup tomato juice

2 tablespoons tomato paste

2 tablespoons fresh oregano, minced, or 1 teaspoon dried

½ teaspoon garlic powder

½ teaspoon dried basil

1 tablespoon oil

1 16-ounce package firm or extra-firm tofu, sliced

The familiar flavors of spaghetti dress up this grilled tofu.

1. Whisk together the tomato juice, tomato paste, oregano, garlic powder, basil, and oil. Marinate tofu, coating well, for at least 30 minutes, preferably longer.

2. Place tofu over medium heat on grill and baste for sauce. Grill for 5–6 minutes on each side, basting frequently with extra sauce.

Orange-Glazed Tofu

Serves 4

2 tablespoons maple syrup

¼ cup orange juice concentrate

1 tablespoon soy sauce

1 tablespoon sweet chili sauce

1 tablespoon olive oil

1 16-ounce package firm or extra-firm tofu, pressed, sliced

The tasty combination of sweet chili sauce and orange juice forms a lovely orange glaze on grilled tofu. Extra sauce makes for a great dip.

1. Whisk together all ingredients except tofu until combined. Cover tofu with sauce mixture and allow to marinate for at least 30 minutes; longer is better.

2. Place tofu on a well-greased grill over medium heat for 5–6 minutes per side, basting frequently with extra sauce.

Sweet and Spicy Kansas City Tofu

Serves 4

1 teaspoon brown sugar

2 teaspoons hot mustard

¼ cup barbecue sauce

1 tablespoon olive oil

1 tablespoon water

1 16-ounce package firm or extra-firm tofu, sliced

Folks in Kansas City love their barbecue. The secret ingredient to Kansas City-style grilling? Spicy mustard paired with sugar. Though tofu may not be a local favorite in Kansas City, it should be—tofu absorbs the sweet and spicy flavors even better than meat.

1. Whisk together all ingredients except tofu until combined. Cover tofu with sauce mixture and allow to marinate for at least 30 minutes; longer is better.

2. Place tofu on a well-greased grill over medium heat for 5–6 minutes per side, basting frequently with extra sauce.

Try It on Seitan

Seitan isn't as absorbent as tofu, so thinner oil-based sauces tend to fall right off. Thicker sauces, such as this Kansas City sauce and others with a barbecue-sauce base (such as Kentucky Bourbon Tofu—see recipe in this chapter), can be basted on seitan as well as tofu. Eliminate the extra water, and increase the marinating time. Seitan needs 1 hour minimum, while tofu, in general, needs about 20 minutes. With both, of course, the longer the better!

Kentucky Bourbon Tofu

Serves 4

3 tablespoons bourbon

1 teaspoon vegan Worcestershire sauce

1 tablespoon molasses

¼ cup barbecue sauce

1 16-ounce package firm or extra-firm tofu, pressed, sliced

Kansas City may be famous for its barbecue, but Kentucky is famous for its bourbon, which goes right into this glazed and grilled tofu. Make sure you have a mint julep in one hand while you watch over this Kentucky-style grilled tofu.

1. Whisk together all ingredients except tofu until combined. Cover tofu with sauce mixture and allow to marinate for at least 30 minutes; longer is better.

2. Place tofu on a well-greased grill over medium heat for 5–6 minutes per side, basting frequently with extra sauce.

Easy Smokehouse Tofu

Serves 4

1 16-ounce package extra-firm tofu, frozen, thawed, pressed, and sliced
1½–2 cups wood chips, any kind

Smoked tofu is delicious on its own, but also tastes delicious in salads and stir-fries, and keeps in the fridge. To add a lovely crust, season your tofu with a dry rub first —try the recipe used in the Texas Hickory-Smoked Seitan (see Chapter 8).

1. Soak wood chips in water for 30–45 minutes. If using a gas grill, preheat only one side or one burner to low heat. If using charcoal, move coals to one side.

2. Wrap wet wood chips in foil, leaving extra space in the packet for air. Poke lots of holes in the foil. Place the wood chip packet over the heat source on your gas grill, or directly on the coals. Place the tofu as far away from the heat as possible.

3. Smoke tofu for 45–60 minutes, adding more soaked wood chips as needed, about every 20–30 minutes.

Freezing Tofu

Pressing tofu works to encourage tofu to soak up a tasty homemade marinade, but if you want an even "meatier" texture, try freezing the tofu first. You'll remove even more liquid. Drain the water, then place the whole block in the freezer. Thaw it out, and then press it normally. Freezing tofu works when you want a meatlike tofu that absorbs lots of flavor, as in this smoked tofu.

Japanese Yaki Dofu in Teriyaki Sauce

Serves 4

⅓ cup soy sauce

¼ cup water

2 tablespoons honey

1 teaspoon garlic powder

1 tablespoon minced fresh ginger

1 16-ounce package firm or extra-firm tofu, sliced

2 teaspoons cornstarch

3 tablespoons water

1 teaspoon sesame oil

¼ cup scallions (optional)

2 tablespoons sesame seeds (optional)

Japan has a long history of grilling, tofu, and grilling tofu. Dengaku Miso Tofu (see this chapter) is one traditional preparation, as is "yaki dofu," a grilled tofu used in many Japanese dishes. This version isn't quite traditional and authentic, but it's delicious nonetheless.

1. Whisk together the soy sauce, water, honey, garlic powder, and ginger. Marinate tofu in sauce for at least 20 minutes; longer is better. Drain tofu and set aside. Reserve extra marinade.

2. Place extra marinade in a small saucepan and simmer over low heat. In a small bowl, whisk together cornstarch and water. Add to simmering marinade, stirring to incorporate. Simmer another 2–3 minutes, until sauce has thickened. Whisk in sesame oil.

3. Place marinated tofu on a well-greased grill over medium heat for 5–6 minutes per side. Serve topped with thickened sauce, and garnish with scallions and sesame seeds, if desired.

Ketchup-Grilled Tofu for Kids

Serves 4

¼ cup pineapple juice

2 tablespoons maple syrup

2 tablespoons ketchup

1 tablespoon soy sauce

1 tablespoon oil

1 16-ounce package firm or extra-firm tofu, sliced

Kids will love this mild grilled tofu with its sweet flavors. Adults might prefer it made with hot sauce in place of the ketchup.

1. Whisk together the pineapple juice, maple syrup, ketchup, soy sauce, and oil. Cover tofu with sauce and allow to marinate for at least 30 minutes; longer is better.

2. Place tofu on a well-greased grill over medium heat for 5–6 minutes per side, basting frequently with extra sauce.

Vietnamese Lemongrass Tofu

Serves 4

3 tablespoons finely minced lemongrass

1 small chili pepper, minced (optional)

4 cloves garlic, minced

2 teaspoons fresh minced ginger or galangal

2 teaspoons brown sugar

1 tablespoon soy sauce

2 tablespoons lime juice

2 teaspoons sesame oil

2 teaspoons peanut oil or olive oil

1 16-ounce package firm or extra-firm tofu, pressed, sliced

When working with lemongrass, use only the lower pale ends of the stalk, which should be softer than the darker green part. Add onions, mushrooms, scallions, or bell peppers to the skewers if you'd like.

1. Use a mortar and pestle to grind together the lemongrass, chili pepper, garlic, and ginger to form a rough paste. Combine with brown sugar, soy sauce, lime juice, and oils to form a marinade. Marinate pressed tofu for at least 30 minutes, covering with sauce.

2. Place tofu on a well-greased grill over medium heat for 5–6 minutes per side.

Nature's Skewers

The stiff green part of lemongrass makes a wonderful natural skewer for grilled foods, and imparts another delicate layer of Southeast Asian flavor to your meal. Here's how: Slice the stiff green upper part of the lemongrass stalks to the desired length, and peel off any loose or brown layers. Larger lemongrass stalks can be sliced in half lengthwise to form two smaller skewers. Try using lemongrass as a skewer in this recipe, with the Easy Sweet Indonesian Seitan Satay (see Chapter 8), or with the Lemon Thyme Tempeh (see Chapter 8). You can also buy lemongrass-flavored bamboo skewers for a similar effect, but they don't look nearly as impressive as these natural skewers.

Easiest Tofu Ever

Serves 4

⅓ cup store-bought salad dressing, barbecue sauce, hoisin sauce, or other marinade sauce

1 16-ounce package firm or extra-firm tofu, pressed, sliced

Sometimes you just want dinner to be ready already! This is for those times. You can skip the usual marinating time here—just brush lots of sauce on while the tofu is on the grill.

1. Coat tofu in dressing or barbecue sauce and place on a hot grill until browned, basting as needed with extra sauce.

Mango Teriyaki Tofu

Serves 4

¼ cup mango nectar or mango juice

¼ cup teriyaki sauce

1 tablespoon olive oil

3 cloves garlic, minced

½ teaspoon sugar

1 16-ounce package firm or extra-firm tofu, sliced

Turn this sweet glazed tofu into tropical skewers by adding pineapple and red bell peppers, perhaps even mango chunks.

1. Whisk together the mango nectar, teriyaki sauce, olive oil, garlic, and sugar. Cover tofu with marinade and allow to marinate for at least 30 minutes; longer is better.

2. Place on a well-greased grill over medium heat for 5–6 minutes per side, basting frequently with extra sauce.

Curried Apricot and Tofu Sosaties

Serves 4

3 cloves garlic, minced
2 tablespoons oil
1 tablespoon curry
½ teaspoon turmeric
3 tablespoons lemon juice
½ cup water
1 tablespoon brown sugar
¼ cup apricot jam
1 16-ounce package tofu, chopped into 1" cubes
25 dried apricots
1 green bell pepper, chopped

Barbecues, called braai, *are serious business in South Africa and have been influenced by a number of other global cuisines. "Sosatie" skewers are usually prepared with lamb, but tofu carries the sweet and spicy flavors just as well. Native South Africans might add prunes to these skewers in place of the apricots.*

1. Sauté garlic in oil for 3–4 minutes, then add curry, turmeric, lemon juice, and water, stirring to combine. Add brown sugar and jam, and simmer for 6–8 minutes, until combined.

2. Marinate the tofu, dried apricots, and bell pepper in the apricot-jam-and-curry sauce for at least 1 hour, preferably 2–3. Sauce will thicken as it cools.

3. Skewer ingredients, packing them tightly together. Place on a well-greased grill, turning once or twice and basting frequently, until veggies are soft and tofu is well cooked, about 10–12 minutes. Serve topped with a little extra marinade.

Chapter 8

Seitan and Tempeh

Seitan Hot Wings

Serves 4

2 tablespoons olive oil
⅝ cup hot sauce, divided
1 tablespoon water
1 tablespoon paprika
1 teaspoon garlic powder
1 teaspoon onion powder
1 16-ounce package prepared seitan, chopped into chunks or thin strips
⅓ cup margarine, slightly melted

These spicy Buffalo-style seitan "wings" are not for the timid. They're gooey and messy, so perhaps best served on a skewer, or with plenty of napkins for sticky fingers. Serve with cold ranch dressing if you want to be traditional, or with mint raita (see Tandoori-Spiced Paneer Skewers with Mint Raita recipe in Chapter 9) for a global flair.

1. Whisk together the olive oil, 2 tablespoons hot sauce, and water, then add paprika, garlic powder, and onion powder. Pour over seitan; marinate for at least 1 hour, preferably longer.

2. Skewer, if needed, and place on a well-greased grill, basting with extra sauce. Grill for 6–7 minutes on each side, or until browned.

3. Whisk together ½ cup hot sauce and melted margarine and coat seitan with sauce. Cool slightly before serving, to allow sauce to thicken.

Lemon Thyme Tempeh

Serves 4

1 8-ounce package tempeh
Water for simmering
¼ cup fresh lemon juice
1 tablespoon olive oil
1 teaspoon sugar
2 teaspoons thyme
1 teaspoon lemon pepper

Fresh lemon juice is a must in this recipe. Garnish with grilled lemon slices and serve with an ice-cold lemonade.

1. Slice tempeh into desired shapes, then simmer in 1–2" of water for 15 minutes. Drain.

2. Whisk together the fresh lemon juice, olive oil, sugar, thyme, and lemon pepper to form a marinade, and cover tempeh in a shallow pan or sealable bag. Allow tempeh to marinate for at least 1 hour, turning as needed to coat thoroughly with marinade.

3. Place tempeh on a well-greased grill and baste with extra marinade. Grill over medium heat for 6–8 minutes, or until done, turning once or twice as needed and basting frequently.

Garnishing with Grilled Lemon Slices

Grilled lemon slices make a bright and beautiful garnish to any summer meal. They look like little bursts of summer sunshine on your plate or on your food. Here's how to do it: Slice a whole lemon widthwise into circular slices about ⅓" thick. Place the slices over medium-low heat on a well-greased grill, and heat them for 3–4 minutes on each side. Grilled lemon slices look beautiful plated on top of a dish such as this one, or place them alongside as a garnish.

Caribbean Jerk-Spiced Tempeh

Serves 2

1 8-ounce package tempeh
1 cup vegetable broth or water
1 tablespoon fresh ginger, minced
2 tablespoons lime juice
2 tablespoons soy sauce
2 tablespoons maple syrup
2 tablespoons olive oil
2 teaspoons thyme
2 teaspoons allspice
½ teaspoon nutmeg or cloves
1 small chili pepper, minced (optional)
½ teaspoon red pepper flakes

Fill a French roll with some Easy Creamy Coleslaw (see Chapter 11) or Louisiana Coleslaw (see Chapter 11) and add several slices of this tempeh. Don't be stingy with the marinade—really slap it on there, as much as you can!

1. Slice tempeh into desired shapes, then simmer in vegetable broth or water on the stovetop for at least 15 minutes.

2. Whisk together remaining ingredients and marinate tempeh for at least 1 hour—the longer the better.

3. Baste tempeh with extra marinade, then place on a well-greased grill for 8–10 minutes, turning once and basting frequently with extra marinade. Serve topped with a spoonful of the remaining marinade on top.

Honey Mustard Grilled Tempeh Triangles

Serves 4

1 8-ounce package tempeh

Water for simmering

2 tablespoons mustard

2 tablespoons honey

2 tablespoons olive oil

1 tablespoon soy sauce

2 tablespoons apple cider vinegar

Simmering the tempeh beforehand keeps it moist and juicy on the grill, allowing it to absorb even more of the sticky honey mustard glaze, so don't skip this important step.

1. Slice tempeh in half widthwise to create two large patties, then slice each patty in half to create four even pieces. Simmer tempeh in 1–2" of water for 15 minutes. Drain.

2. Whisk together remaining ingredients to form a marinade, and transfer to a shallow pan or sealable bag. Add tempeh and allow to marinate for at least 1 hour, covering and turning occasionally.

3. Grill over medium heat for 6–8 minutes, or until done, basting occasionally with extra sauce.

Easy Grilled Seitan

Serves 4

1 16-ounce package prepared seitan

½ cup barbecue sauce

Use a good quality barbecue sauce, since that's where the flavor in this recipe comes from.

1. Marinate seitan in barbecue sauce for at least 1 hour, preferably 2–3.

2. Brush extra sauce onto the seitan and place on a well-greased grill for 6–7 minutes on each side, basting frequently with extra sauce.

Easy Grilled Tempeh

Serves 2

1 8-ounce block tempeh
1 cup vegetable broth or water
½ cup barbecue sauce

Though tempeh works wonderfully on the grill, it doesn't pick up flavors as easily as tofu or even seitan, so a longer marinating time works best. Presimmering it in broth gives it a softer texture and makes it a bit more absorbent.

1. If your tempeh is thicker than 1", slice it in half width-wise. Slice it again into desired shapes. Triangles or strips about 1" thick work well, or slice into patty-sized squares to use as veggie burgers.

2. Simmer tempeh in vegetable broth on the stovetop for at least 15 minutes.

3. Marinate tempeh in barbecue sauce for at least 1 hour; 2–3 is better.

4. Place tempeh on a well-greased grill for 8–10 minutes, turning once and basting frequently with extra sauce.

Texas Hickory-Smoked Seitan

Serves 4

1 16-ounce package prepared seitan

2 teaspoons sweet paprika

1 teaspoon sea salt or kosher salt

1 teaspoon brown sugar

1 teaspoon chili powder

1 teaspoon cumin

½ teaspoon cayenne pepper

1 teaspoon fresh ground black pepper

1½–2 cups hickory wood chips

Barbecue sauce for serving

With this look-alike and smell-alike recipe, you can fool omnivores into thinking they're eating Texas brisket. What part of the animal is a "brisket" anyway?

1. Slice seitan into thin, wide slabs. Combine remaining ingredients except wood chips and barbecue sauce and rub thoroughly onto seitan. Allow to sit for a few minutes to absorb spices, then rub again.

2. Soak wood chips in water for 30–45 minutes. If using a gas grill, preheat only one side or one burner to low heat. If using charcoal, move coals to one side.

3. Wrap wet wood chips in foil, leaving extra space in the packet for air. Poke lots of holes in the foil. Place the wood chip packet over the heat source on your gas grill, or directly on the coals. Place the seitan away from the heat. Soaked wood chips can also be placed directly on coals, without foil.

4. Smoke seitan for at least 1 hour and up to 2 hours, adding more soaked wood chips as needed. Top it off with your favorite barbecue sauce and devour hungrily.

For the Barbecue Enthusiast Who Has Everything

Wood chips make an excellent present for the grill lover who has everything. Bring along an assortment of chips as a hostess gift in lieu of the usual wine bottle. Mesquite, apple, and hickory woods are the most popular, but the gourmet grill chef might prefer one of the mulberry, maple, cherry, or whiskey- or bourbon-infused chips on the market. No-fuss cooks might prefer the tinned chips, which are ready to go and can be placed right on the grill.

Taco-Spiced Tempeh with Chipotle Mayonnaise

Serves 4

1 8-ounce package tempeh

1 cup vegetable broth or water

2 tablespoons lime juice

2 tablespoons soy sauce

1 tablespoon olive oil

1 packet vegetarian taco seasoning

½ cup mayonnaise

1 heaping tablespoon minced chipotle pepper in adobo

2 teaspoons adobo sauce

½ teaspoon garlic salt

Use this Mexican-inspired tempeh to make tacos, open-faced tostadas, or sandwiches, or just eat it up with a fork the second it's cool enough.

1. Slice tempeh into desired shapes, then simmer in vegetable broth or water on the stovetop for at least 15 minutes.

2. Whisk together the lime juice, soy sauce, olive oil, and ½ packet of taco seasoning. Marinate tempeh for at least 1 hour.

3. Remove tempeh from marinade and sprinkle with remaining ½ packet of taco seasoning. Place on a well-greased grill for 8–10 minutes, turning once or twice and brushing once or twice with extra marinade.

4. Whisk together mayonnaise, chipotle pepper, adobo sauce, and garlic salt and serve on top of grilled tempeh.

Pineapple-Glazed Tempeh with Pineapples

Serves 4

1 8-ounce package tempeh
Water for simmering
2 tablespoons olive oil
2 tablespoons soy sauce
1 tablespoon apple cider vinegar
3 tablespoons pineapple preserves
1 medium pineapple, chopped into 1" chunks

Pineapple, a traditional grill favorite, lends its flavor well to grilled tempeh.

1. Slice tempeh into 1" chunks, then simmer in 1–2" of water for 15 minutes. Drain.

2. Whisk together the olive oil, soy sauce, apple cider vinegar, and pineapple preserves to form a marinade, and cover tempeh in a shallow pan or sealable bag. Allow tempeh to marinate for at least 1 hour, turning as needed to coat thoroughly with marinade.

3. Place tempeh and pineapple chunks on soaked skewers, and baste tempeh with extra marinade. Grill over medium heat for 6–8 minutes or until done, turning once or twice as needed. Baste tempeh with extra marinade 1–2 minutes before done.

Tangy Memphis Tempeh

Serves 4

1 8-ounce package tempeh

Water for simmering

1 tablespoon paprika

2 teaspoons brown sugar

½ teaspoon garlic powder

½ teaspoon onion powder

½ teaspoon mustard powder

½ teaspoon salt

¼ teaspoon black pepper

¼ teaspoon cayenne pepper, or more to taste

¼ cup sweet barbecue sauce

3 tablespoons ketchup

2 tablespoons white or apple cider vinegar

Oil for brushing

Memphis is known for its spicy dry rubs and thin vinegar barbecue sauces, which are basted on just before the cooking process is done.

1. Slice tempeh into desired shapes, then simmer in 1–2" of water for 15 minutes. Drain.

2. Combine paprika, brown sugar, garlic powder, onion powder, mustard powder, salt, black pepper, and cayenne pepper. Transfer to a large resealable plastic bag and add tempeh, shaking gently to coat. Allow tempeh to sit for at least 30 minutes in dry rub mixture.

3. Whisk together barbecue sauce, ketchup, and vinegar and set aside.

4. Brush tempeh with oil, then rub with dry rub spice mixture. Place on a well-greased grill over medium heat for 6–8 minutes, or until done, turning once or twice as needed. Baste with barbecue sauce mixture 1–2 minutes before done, then serve with sauce on the side.

Try It Smoked

Smoked tempeh can be prepared much in the same way as smoked tofu. To make Memphis-Smoked Tempeh, presimmer the tempeh, rub it with the seasoning mix, then smoke it for 20–30 minutes. Baste with sauce, then grill for just a minute or two to finish it off.

Easy Sweet Indonesian Seitan Satay

Serves 4

| 1 tablespoon vegan curry paste |
| 1/3 cup peanut butter |
| 2 teaspoons soy sauce |
| 2 teaspoons brown sugar |
| 2/3 cup coconut milk |
| 1 16-ounce package prepared seitan |

For less sweet, more heat, add extra curry paste and a fresh minced chili. Make sure your curry paste is vegan, as some brands contain shrimp or fish sauce.

1. Warm all ingredients except seitan on the stovetop over low heat for just a few minutes, stirring frequently until combined.

2. Slice seitan thinly, about ½" thick. Marinate in satay sauce for at least 1 hour. Skewer seitan, then place on a well-greased grill for about 4–5 minutes, turning once. Serve with extra sauce.

Raspberry Tarragon Tempeh

Serves 4

1 8-ounce package tempeh

Water for simmering

1 tablespoon lemon juice

1 shallot, minced

⅓ cup raspberry vinegar

2 tablespoons raspberry preserves

1 teaspoon tarragon

2 tablespoons olive oil

Tempeh goes gourmet on the grill with this raspberry-tarragon combination. Triangles present best, but any shape will do.

1. Slice tempeh in half widthwise to create 2 large patties, then slice each patty in half to create 4 even pieces. Simmer tempeh in 1–2" of water for 15 minutes. Drain.

2. Combine remaining ingredients, whisking to combine. Marinate tempeh for at least 1 hour.

3. Place tempeh on a well-greased grill for 8–10 minutes, turning once and basting with extra marinade. Drizzle with any leftover marinade just before serving.

Bulgogi Seitan Skewers

Serves 4

3 cloves garlic, minced

⅓ cup soy sauce

1 tablespoon hoisin sauce

1 tablespoon rice vinegar or rice wine

4 teaspoons sugar

1 teaspoon onion powder

1 teaspoon garlic powder

1 onion, chopped into chunks

2 tablespoons sesame oil

2 teaspoons black pepper

2 tablespoons fresh ginger, minced

1 16-ounce package prepared seitan

Korean food is filled with unmistakably strong flavors, and this vegetarian bulgogi is no exception.

1. Whisk together all ingredients, except seitan, to form a marinade. Add thinly sliced seitan, cover with the liquid, and marinate for at least 3 hours, preferably overnight.

2. Carefully skewer seitan and place on a well-greased grill for 6–7 minutes on each side, brushing frequently with extra marinade.

Maple Jack Seitan

Serves 4

¼ cup maple syrup
¼ cup Jack Daniel's whiskey
¼ cup barbecue sauce
2 tablespoons vegan margarine
1 16-ounce package prepared seitan, sliced into thin slabs

Anytime you use alcohol around fire, be prepared for flare-ups. Baste lightly, and watch your eyebrows.

1. Whisk together maple syrup, whiskey, barbecue sauce, and margarine on the stovetop until margarine has melted and ingredients are combined.

2. Place seitan in syrup mixture and chill for at least 1 hour.

3. Baste seitan generously with sauce, then place on a well-greased grill for 6–7 minutes on each side, brushing frequently with extra sauce. Baste again one minute before taking off the grill.

Smoked Whiskey "Ribs"

As an alternative, smoke this seitan instead of grilling it. Use the same method as with the Texas Hickory-Smoked Seitan (see recipe in this chapter), basting with a light layer of sauce every 30 minutes or so.

Prime Seitan Au Jus with Horseradish Hollandaise

Serves 4

1 cup water

1 vegetarian beef-flavored bouillon cube

½ cup red wine

1 clove garlic, minced

½ teaspoon salt, plus additional for seasoning

¼ teaspoon fresh black pepper, plus additional for seasoning

1 16-ounce package prepared seitan

1 tablespoon butter or margarine

Oil for brushing

¼ cup mayonnaise

1 teaspoon prepared horseradish (more if you really like horseradish!)

2 tablespoons chopped fresh chives

Serve on a French roll to make a sandwich, or slice it up and just eat it as is.

1. Combine water and bouillon cube in a large skillet over low heat until combined, then add red wine, garlic, salt, and pepper. Simmer seitan in mixture for 15 minutes. Allow to cool.

2. Remove seitan and reheat red wine mixture. Add butter or margarine, and heat until thickened and reduced to about ¼ cup. Set aside.

3. Brush seitan with oil and grill for 6–7 minutes on each side, brushing once on each side with extra red wine sauce.

4. Whisk together mayonnaise, horseradish, and chives and season lightly with salt and pepper to make horseradish hollandaise. Serve seitan with red wine sauce and horseradish hollandaise.

Orange Garlic Tempeh

Serves 4

1 8-ounce package tempeh
1 cup vegetable broth or water
¼ cup orange marmalade
2 tablespoons olive oil
1 tablespoon soy sauce
1 tablespoon apple cider vinegar
4 cloves garlic, minced

Orange marmalade caramelizes on the grill to create an attractive and shiny glaze for this dish inspired by Asian Orange Chicken.

1. Slice tempeh into desired shapes, then simmer in vegetable broth or water on the stovetop for at least 15 minutes.

2. Whisk together orange marmalade, olive oil, soy sauce, vinegar, and garlic. Marinate tempeh for at least 1 hour.

3. Remove tempeh from marinade and place on a well-greased grill for 8–10 minutes, turning once or twice and brushing frequently with extra marinade. Serve smeared generously with any remaining marinade.

Drunken Seitan with Beer Sauce

Serves 4

½ cup beer
½ cup barbecue sauce
2 tablespoons steak sauce
1 tablespoon brown sugar
1 teaspoon garlic powder
½ teaspoon onion powder
¾ teaspoon salt
½ teaspoon pepper
1 16-ounce package prepared seitan

Cooking this dish for kids? Try it with root beer!

1. Simmer together all ingredients, except seitan, in a small saucepan for 4–5 minutes, just until combined and heated through.

2. Marinate seitan in sauce for at least 1 hour, being sure to coat with sauce.

3. Grill seitan, either on skewers or directly on the grill, until lightly browned, about 6–7 minutes on each side.

How Do You Like Your Seitan?

Seitan works well on the grill, picking up delicious smoky flavors. Skewer chunks of seitan just as you would tofu or vegetables. Or try flattening homemade seitan and placing it directly on the grill. Unlike tofu, seitan has an uneven texture, which means it's likely to get some charred edges. But don't worry—burned ends are a grilled delicacy. Just place it over lower or indirect heat if your bumpy seitan is getting too blackened in some parts. Remember—the smaller the slices or chunks, the more surface area, and that means more sauce absorption and smoky flavor. Some recipes, such as the Bulgogi Seitan Skewers (see Chapter 8) and Easy Sweet Indonesian Seitan Satay (see Chapter 8) work much better on thinly sliced seitan.

Teriyaki Tempeh Kebabs

Serves 4

²⁄₃ cup water

¼ cup soy sauce

3 tablespoons brown sugar

2 scallions, minced

2 teaspoons fresh minced ginger

1 tablespoon cornstarch dissolved in
¼ cup water

1 8-ounce package tempeh

1 cup vegetable broth or water

12 chunks pineapple

1 tomato, chopped into chunks

1 green bell pepper, chopped

Pineapples, tomatoes, and bell peppers go with a salty and sweet teriyaki tempeh for an attractive (and tasty!) barbecue kebab.

1. Simmer water with soy sauce, brown sugar, scallions, and ginger over low heat, just until sugar is dissolved. Add dissolved cornstarch and simmer until thickened. Set marinade aside.

2. Slice tempeh into 1" chunks, then simmer in vegetable broth on the stovetop for at least 15 minutes.

3. Place tempeh in teriyaki marinade, covering well with sauce. Marinate for at least 1 hour—the longer the better.

4. Arrange pineapples, tomato chunks, bell pepper, and tempeh on a skewers and brush all ingredients with marinade.

5. Place skewers on a greased grill for 8–10 minutes, or until well-cooked, turning as needed and basting with extra sauce.

Chapter 9

Miscellaneous Mains

Easy Pesto Pizzas on Pita Bread

Serves 2

2 pita breads

Olive oil for brushing

⅓ cup prepared pesto

6 artichoke hearts, chopped

½ cup grated mozzarella, provolone, or other cheese

If you don't want to deal with pizza dough, try making individual grilled pizzas using pita bread as a base. Follow this super-easy recipe, or experiment with your own traditional pizza toppings. Try it with mini pitas for an appetizer!

1. Brush pitas with olive oil on one side and place on a work surface, oiled side down. Spread pesto on each pita round, then top with chopped artichoke hearts and cheese.

2. Place on a well-greased grill for 4–5 minutes, or until bread is toasted and cheese has melted.

Calzone Tre Formaggio

Serves 4

Cornmeal for dusting

1½ pounds store-bought pizza dough

8 ounces pizza sauce

1 cup grated mozzarella cheese

½ cup grated Parmesan cheese

1 cup ricotta cheese

1 cup loosely packed fresh basil leaves, shredded

2 tablespoons fresh oregano leaves or 2 teaspoons dried

Red pepper flakes to taste

Salt and fresh ground black pepper to taste

1 egg yolk, beaten

A calzone is a folded, stuffed piece of pizza dough that is baked until the crust is brown. They're excellent on the grill.

1. Spread cornmeal on a flat work surface. Divide pizza dough into 4 even balls. Roll each ball out into a round, about 6" in diameter.

2. Mix the pizza sauce, cheeses, basil, oregano, and red pepper flakes. Season with salt and pepper. Spread ¼ of the filling on the lower ½ of 1 dough round. Fold the half that is not sauced over the filling and crimp the edges with a fork. Repeat with other 3 dough rounds.

3. Place calzones on a heavy baking pan or pizza stone. Brush the calzones with egg yolk and use a fork to prick the top in two places. Place on a covered grill for 8–10 minutes, or until brown and bubbly.

Dough-Making Basics

Dough for pizza and calzones is readily available at supermarkets and bakeries. If you buy your dough, you'll save a great deal of time—aside from the original process of mixing and kneading, dough has to rise for 1 hour, then after rolling, rise for another 15–20 minutes. Give yourself and your family a break and buy it. You can also use fresh or frozen bread dough, which is similar to pizza dough.

Stuffed Poblanos

Serves 6

1 15-ounce can black beans, drained
¾ cup cooked rice
½ cup TVP, rehydrated
¼ cup salsa
½ teaspoon chili powder
¼ teaspoon salt
6 large poblano peppers, sliced in half

They aren't quite traditional chili rellenos, but the beauty of this recipe is that everything can be prepared outdoors, as long as you've got some leftover rice on hand. Serve with sour cream.

1. Mash beans slightly and combine with rice, rehydrated TVP, salsa, chili powder, and salt.

2. Place halved poblanos on the grill for 8–10 minutes, or until lightly charred.

3. Remove from grill and fill with bean and rice mixture. Return to the grill for another 4–5 minutes, until heated through.

Feta or Pesto Napoleon Antipasto

Serves 4

1 medium eggplant, sliced into ½"-thick rounds

1 yellow squash, sliced into long strips

1 zucchini, sliced into long strips

1 red or yellow bell pepper, sliced

2 medium tomatoes, sliced into ½"-thick rounds

¼ cup olive oil

2 tablespoons lemon juice

½ teaspoon parsley

½ teaspoon oregano

¼ teaspoon crushed red pepper flakes

Salt and pepper

1 tablespoon balsamic vinegar

2 tablespoons chopped fresh basil

¼ cup feta cheese crumbles (or ¼ cup vegan pesto, if preparing vegan)

For these antipasto vegetables stacked Napoleon-style, you can leave off the feta for the vegans and instead add a large dab of vegan pesto topped off with pine nuts. For a variation, stack it all on top of a slice of grilled polenta.

1. Combine eggplant, yellow squash, zucchini, bell pepper, and tomatoes in a large bowl. In a separate small bowl, whisk together the olive oil, lemon juice, parsley, oregano, and red pepper flakes. Add the olive oil mix to the veggies, tossing to coat well. Allow to sit for at least 45 minutes; over 1 hour is better.

2. Season vegetables lightly with salt and pepper, then place on a well-greased grill for just a few minutes per side until tender but not too soft.

3. To assemble stacks, place eggplant rounds on plate, layer tomatoes on top, then place pepper and squash strips in stacks on top. Drizzle with balsamic vinegar and sprinkle with fresh basil and crumbled feta.

The Minimalist Pizza

Serves 4

¼ cup cornmeal

1 pound fresh pizza dough

1 cup tomato sauce

12 fresh basil leaves, shredded

8 ounces fresh mozzarella, coarsely grated

Simplify your life: mozzarella, tomato sauce, fresh basil, and nothing else. If you're not in the mood for Zen, a shake of oregano or red pepper flakes adds extra spice.

1. Sprinkle the cornmeal on a flat work surface and roll out the dough over it.

2. Spread the tomato sauce evenly on the dough; the shredded basil, then the mozzarella.

3. Place dough on a pizza stone and place in grill. Bake until the crust is brown and the topping bubbles.

Grilled Polenta with Avocado Pico de Gallo

Serves 4

6½ cups water
2 cups cornmeal
3 tablespoons vegan margarine
1½ teaspoons garlic powder
¼ cup nutritional yeast
½ teaspoon salt
1 large avocado, diced
1 medium tomato, diced small
⅓ cup onion, diced small
2 cloves garlic, minced
1 small jalapeño or serrano chili pepper, diced small
¼ cup chopped fresh cilantro
1 tablespoon fresh lemon or lime juice
¼ teaspoon sea salt, or to taste

Grilling Polenta

Yes, you can grill up store-bought polenta in the tube. Just slice, brush with olive oil, and grill. Feeling lazy? Top it off with store-bought salsa, olive tapenade, pesto, a green chili sauce (yum!), or a balsamic or red wine reduction sauce.

Pairing grilled polenta with this fresh avocado pico de gallo makes for a wonderfully bright and colorful summer dish. Serve it with Spice-Crusted Halloumi Bites (see Chapter 2), or Crisped Camembert and Mango Quesadillas (see Chapter 2) for a Latin-fusion meal. The wine? A Zinfandel or another Argentinean red, or for a white, Pinot grigio.

1. Bring the water to a boil on the stovetop, then slowly add cornmeal, stirring to combine. Reduce heat to low and cook for 20 minutes, stirring frequently and scraping the bottom of the pot to prevent sticking and burning. Cornmeal/polenta is done when it is thick and sticky.

2. Stir in margarine, garlic powder, nutritional yeast, and salt. Place in a small, lightly greased loaf pan and chill until very firm, about 1–2 hours.

3. To prepare pico de gallo, combine avocado, tomato, onion, garlic, jalapeño pepper, and cilantro. Drizzle with lime juice and season with sea salt, gently tossing to combine.

4. Slice polenta 1" thick and brush with olive oil. Sprinkle with extra garlic powder and place on a greased grill over medium heat. Grill, turning only once (be careful!), for about 4–5 minutes per side. Serve topped with avocado pico de gallo.

Broccoli and Tofu Lettuce Wraps with Hoisin Sauce

Serves 4

1 head broccoli, quartered

Oil for brushing

2 tablespoons hoisin sauce

1 tablespoon water

1 teaspoon fresh ginger, minced

8 large iceberg lettuce, Boston lettuce, or napa cabbage leaves

1 cup bean sprouts

¼ cup chopped scallions

1 batch Hoisin-Glazed Tofu (see Chapter 7), chopped small

Juice from one lime

¼ cup chopped fresh cilantro (optional)

Western palates tend to find sweet and pungent hoisin sauce quite tasty—in small quantities. If you find the hoisin flavor overpowering, dilute the sauce mixture a bit with water or oil. Try it with the Vietnamese Lemongrass Tofu (see recipe in Chapter 7), or the Mojito-Marinated Tofu (see recipe in Chapter 7).

1. Brush broccoli with oil. Place directly on the grill over low or indirect heat for about 10 minutes, turning once or twice, until lightly charred. Remove from grill and chop small.

2. Whisk together hoisin sauce, water, and ginger and toss with broccoli.

3. Arrange lettuce leaves on a flat work surface and place bean sprouts and scallions in each. Top with chopped tofu and broccoli. Drizzle with a bit of lime juice and garnish with chopped fresh cilantro, if desired. Wrap and enjoy!

Herb-Stuffed Tomatoes with Gruyere

Serves 4

4 large beefsteak tomatoes

4 cloves Roasted Garlic (see recipe in Chapter 2), mashed

2 tablespoons fresh basil, shredded

½ cup bread crumbs

Salt and pepper to taste

4 teaspoons Gruyère cheese, freshly grated

4 teaspoons olive oil

¼ cup fresh parsley, chopped

This delectable side dish goes with any entrée. You can stuff the tomatoes a day in advance and keep them in the refrigerator.

1. Rinse the tomatoes and pat them dry on paper towels. Cut the very tops off the tomatoes. Using a melon baller, remove and discard some of the juice and seeds from inside the tomatoes.

2. Mix together the garlic, basil, bread crumbs, salt, and pepper. Add the cheese.

3. Stuff the tomatoes with the bread-crumb-and-cheese mixture, pressing it down into the tomatoes. Place each tomato on a piece of heavy-duty aluminum foil and drizzle with olive oil.

4. Place tomatoes on the grill with lid closed for about 10 minutes, or until the tomatoes are soft and the tops are browned. Sprinkle chopped parsley over the tops of the tomatoes.

Tacos al Carbon

Serves 4

4 flour tortillas

1 batch Texas Hickory-Smoked Seitan (see Chapter 8), cut into thin strips

1 recipe Roasted Peppers on the Grill (see Chapter 5), cut into strips

⅓ cup Fired-Up Salsa Verde (see recipe in Chapter 2)

¼ cup sour cream

¼ cup guacamole (optional)

Lime wedges and chopped cilantro for garnish (optional)

Tacos al Carbon are nothing more than fajitas, really—a classic case of Texas meets Mexico, or in this case, seitan meets Tex-Mex. Set everything out and allow diners to assemble their own fajitas.

1. Warm flour tortillas on the grill for just 30 seconds on each side, until soft and pliable.

2. To serve, pile several strips of the smoked seitan and roasted red peppers in the center of each tortilla. Top with salsa verde, sour cream, and guacamole (if desired). Squeeze a lime wedge over each and add a light sprinkle of cilantro. Wrap and eat!

Eggplant Pizza Rounds

Serves 4

1 large eggplant, sliced ¾–1" thick

Oil for brushing

1 teaspoon garlic salt

½–⅔ cup pizza sauce

½ teaspoon Italian seasoning

½ cup mozzarella cheese

Optional pizza toppings: pineapple, sliced olives, vegetarian pepperoni

No crust, just veggies topped with pizza sauce, cheese, and Italian spices.

1. Brush eggplant slices with oil on both sides, and sprinkle with garlic salt. Place on grill and cook for 3–4 minutes, until tender but not too soft.

2. Carefully spread a thin layer of pizza sauce on each slice, then sprinkle with Italian seasonings and mozzarella cheese. Place any additional pizza toppings on top of the cheese.

3. Return eggplant pizzas to the grill and heat for another 2–3 minutes, until cheese melts.

Prepping Eggplants

To enhance the flavor of your eggplants, remove a bit of their bitterness and moisture before grilling. Place an eggplant slice on a paper towel and salt it liberally. Put another paper towel over it and top with another slice of eggplant. Salt this slice and repeat the process until all of the slices have been salted and stacked between paper towels. Let this eggplant tower sit for about 30 minutes, then take out the slices and wipe them off. Now they're ready for the grill.

Seriously Hobo Hobo Packets

Serves 1

Handful frozen French fries or tater tots, thawed

1 veggie burger patty, torn into chunks

¼ cup frozen mixed vegetables, thawed and diced

1 tablespoon vegan margarine

1 tablespoon ketchup or barbecue sauce

Salt and pepper to taste

Some people like to cook, others like to thaw things in the microwave. If you're the latter, these completely un-fancy foil packets ought to keep you happy!

1. Prepare a large square of aluminum foil with non-stick spray. Place thawed French fries or tater tots in the center of the foil, and place veggie burger and thawed veggies on top. Dot with margarine, drizzle with ketchup, and season with salt and pepper.

2. Wrap foil packets tightly and place on the grill for 10–12 minutes, turning once.

Cajun-Rubbed Portobello Caps

Serves 4

2 tablespoons olive or canola oil

2 teaspoons vegan Worcestershire sauce

4 portobello mushroom caps, stems removed

1½ tablespoons paprika

1 teaspoon cayenne pepper

½ teaspoon pepper

½ teaspoon thyme

½ teaspoon oregano

2 teaspoons garlic powder

2 teaspoons onion powder

1 teaspoon salt

These generously spiced portobellos will fill your mouth with the down-home taste of Louisiana. Spicy Cajun food pairs best with a cold beer, rather than a delicate wine.

1. Whisk together oil and Worcestershire sauce and baste mushrooms on both sides.

2. Combine remaining ingredients, and rub mushroom caps well, using as much of the spice blend as will stick.

3. Grill mushrooms over medium heat for 5–6 minutes on each side, or until soft and cooked through.

Grilled Apple Cheddar Pizza

Serves 4

1 12-ounce can ready-made pizza dough, room temperature

2 tablespoons olive oil

⅓ cup barbecue sauce

2 large or 3 medium apples, very thinly sliced

½ red onion, sliced into thin rings

1 cup Cheddar, Swiss, or pepper jack cheese, grated

Kids, grown-ups, and foodies—everyone loves this recipe! Top it off with some vegetarian bacon bits, or add in some caramelized onions or a sprinkle of cinnamon, for that extra touch.

1. Roll dough out to ⅛–¼" thick and lightly brush one side with oil. Place on grill, oil-side down, over low or indirect heat. Grill dough for 3–4 minutes, then carefully remove from heat.

2. Spread a layer of barbecue sauce over the grilled side of the dough, then arrange apple and onion slices over the sauce, and top evenly with cheese.

3. Return pizza to the grill for another 4–5 minutes, until cheese has melted.

Tandoori-Spiced Paneer Skewers with Mint Raita

Serves 4 as a side dish or 2 as an entrée

1 cup plain yogurt, divided (½ cup may be lemon yogurt, if you prefer)

1 tablespoon lemon juice

1 tablespoon tandoori spice blend

½ teaspoon garlic powder

½ teaspoon ginger powder

¼ teaspoon salt

8 ounces paneer, chopped into 1" cubes

⅓ cup chopped fresh mint

1 tablespoon lime juice

½ teaspoon minced chili (optional)

3 tablespoons minced or grated cucumber

Who needs chicken tikka masala? Paneer is even better. The cheese softens while picking up a crispy charred crust and a lovely reddish orange color from all the spices. Prepare the raita well in advance, if possible, to allow the flavors to blend.

1. Whisk together ½ cup plain yogurt with lemon juice, tandoori spice, garlic powder, ginger powder, and salt. Pour over paneer to cover and allow to marinate for at least 1 hour.

2. Combine ½ cup plain or lemon yogurt with fresh mint, lime juice, chili (if used), and cucumber. If time permits, allow to chill for at least 30 minutes.

3. Place paneer on skewers, and baste again with sauce. Grill over medium-low heat for 6–8 minutes, turning to lightly char all sides evenly. Serve with mint raita.

Make It Vegan

Soy yogurt is available just about everywhere these days and will work just fine in this recipe. A well-pressed tofu will pick up the same bright colors and grill marks as the paneer, and even seitan can be marinated and grilled in this tandoori-inspired sauce.

Vegetable and Cheese-Stuffed Calzones

Serves 4

½ cup cornmeal

1½ pounds pizza dough

4 tablespoons olive oil

1 medium zucchini, sliced thinly

1 roasted red pepper, cut into strips

4 scallions, outside paper removed from bottoms, chopped

8 cherry tomatoes, halved

1 teaspoon dried rosemary

1 teaspoon dried oregano

1 teaspoon red pepper flakes, or to taste

Salt to taste

4 ounces Gorgonzola cheese, crumbled

The veggies and cheeses in this recipe can be replaced with others you have on hand.

1. Spread the cornmeal on a flat work surface. Divide the pizza dough into 4 equal balls. Roll out each ball of dough to about 6–7" in diameter.

2. Heat the olive oil in a large frying pan and add the zucchini, pepper, scallions, tomatoes, rosemary, oregano, and pepper flakes. Season with salt to taste. Sauté for 5 minutes, leaving the vegetables crisp.

3. Spread the vegetables on the bottom half of each dough circle. Crumble the cheese on top of the vegetables. Close each calzone and crimp shut with a fork.

4. Bake calzones in a covered grill for 5–8 minutes or until golden brown and very hot.

Easy Kids' Kebabs

Serves 4

20 pineapple chunks

20 grape or cherry tomatoes

1 head broccoli, chopped into florets

¼ cup ketchup

1 teaspoon brown sugar

1 teaspoon mustard

All of the flavors in these simple kebabs are familiar to kids, but you can vary the veggies according to your family favorites—sweet potato chunks or even a few torn bread pieces would work. Add tofu or seitan for a protein source.

1. Place pineapple chunks, tomatoes, and broccoli florets on skewers (or substitute other vegetables your kids like).

2. Whisk together ketchup, sugar, and mustard and lightly brush vegetables with sauce.

3. Place on a well-greased grill, turning and basting until vegetables are well cooked, about 6–8 minutes. Serve with extra sauce for dipping.

Indian-Spiced Polenta with Mango Chutney

Serves 4

1 ripe mango, peeled and chopped

1 large tart apple, peeled, cored, and chopped small

½ cup white raisins (sultanas)

½ cup apple cider vinegar

¼ cup brown sugar

1 tablespoon fresh minced ginger

4 teaspoons Madras curry powder, divided

1 teaspoon salt, divided

6½ cups vegetable broth or water

2 cups cornmeal

2 teaspoons cumin

3 tablespoons vegan margarine

Olive oil for brushing

1 tablespoon chili powder

½ teaspoon cayenne pepper, or to taste (optional)

Who says Indian food has to be, well, Indian? Indian spices go beautifully with Italian grilled polenta. Substitute the homemade mango chutney with store-bought, if you prefer.

1. Mix together the mango, apple, raisins, vinegar, brown sugar, ginger, 2 teaspoons curry powder, and ½ teaspoon salt in a saucepan. Bring to a boil on the stovetop and simmer for 15 minutes, or until sugar melts. Allow to cool before serving, as chutney will thicken as it cools. Set aside.

2. Bring the vegetable broth or water to a boil on the stovetop, then slowly add cornmeal, stirring to combine. Reduce heat to low, and cook for 20 minutes, stirring frequently and scraping the bottom of the pot to prevent sticking and burning. Stir in cumin and remaining two teaspoons curry powder the last 2–3 minutes of cooking. Polenta is done when it is thick and sticky.

3. Stir in margarine and remaining ½ teaspoon salt. Place in a small, lightly greased loaf pan and chill until very firm, about 1–2 hours.

4. Slice polenta 1" thick and brush with olive oil. Sprinkle with chili powder and cayenne pepper and place on a well-greased grill over medium heat. Grill, carefully turning only once, for about 4–5 minutes per side.

5. Top with the mango chutney and serve.

Grilled Stuffed Tomatoes with Lemon Parsley Orzo

Serves 6

⅔ cup orzo, cooked according to package directions

2 teaspoons olive oil

2 tablespoons chopped fresh parsley

2 tablespoons lemon juice

½ teaspoon garlic powder

Salt and pepper to taste

6 large beefsteak tomatoes

⅓ cup seasoned bread crumbs

Use fresh, bright red vine-ripened tomatoes in this recipe.

1. Combine cooked orzo with olive oil, parsley, lemon juice, garlic powder, salt, and pepper.

2. Prepare tomatoes by slicing off the top and gently scooping out the soft interior. Carefully spoon orzo mixture into tomatoes, filling them to the top and mounding slightly.

3. Top stuffed tomatoes with bread crumbs and place on a well-greased grill. Cover and allow to cook for 8–10 minutes.

Grilling Tips for Stuffed Tomatoes

Stuffed tomatoes can be placed directly on the grill. If you find them tumbling a bit, you can wrap them loosely in foil. Or take a square of aluminum foil, roll it up, then twist it. Shape it into a ring of similar diameter to your tomatoes and place tomatoes in the foil ring to help them stay upright.

Mexi-Korean Kimchi Tacos

Serves 4

8 corn tortillas

1 batch Bulgogi Seitan Skewers (see Chapter 8), sliced thin

¼ cup vegan kimchi, or to taste

¼ cup chopped fresh cilantro

1 cup shredded iceberg lettuce

Read the label to make sure your kimchi brand is vegan. Some are, some aren't. Korean kimchi is a bit of an acquired taste, so start with just a little if you're new to the flavor.

1. Warm corn tortillas on the grill for about 1 minute, just until pliable.

2. Fill corn tortillas with bulgogi slices, a bit of kimchi, cilantro, and shredded lettuce and serve.

Salsa Verde and Grilled Zucchini Burritos

Serves 4

1 15-ounce can black beans, drained

2 teaspoons lime juice

¼ cup cilantro, chopped

¼ cup Fired-Up Salsa Verde (see Chapter 2)

2 zucchini, sliced into strips

Olive oil for brushing

2 teaspoons cumin

¼ teaspoon cayenne pepper (optional)

¼ teaspoon salt or kosher salt

4 large flour tortillas

Use up a summer bumper crop of zucchini by piling it into these filling green burritos.

1. Mash together the black beans and lime juice until beans are partially mashed, then add in the cilantro and salsa verde.

2. Brush zucchini strips with olive oil and season with cumin, cayenne pepper (if desired), and salt. Place on the grill until cooked and softened, about 6–7 minutes on each side.

3. Place the flour tortillas on the grill for 10–20 seconds, just to soften them up, then remove from the grill. Place a portion of the bean mixture on each tortilla and top with grilled zucchini.

4. Fold in the sides of the flour tortillas, then roll up to form a burrito. Wrap in aluminum foil and place on the grill until heated through.

Mushroom and Goat Cheese Calzones

Serves 4

½ cup cornmeal

1½ pounds pizza dough

1 cup mushrooms, stemmed and chopped

2 tablespoons olive oil

4 fresh sage leaves, shredded

8 slices vegetarian pepperoni substitute, chopped (optional)

4 ounces goat cheese, at room temperature

A savory grilled calzone always goes best with a cold beer in hand. Just leave out the vegetarian pepperoni if your grocer doesn't stock it.

1. Sprinkle the cornmeal on a flat work surface. Divide the pizza dough into 4 equal balls. Roll out each ball into a round about 6–7" across.

2. Sauté the mushrooms in the olive oil and add sage. Cook for 5 minutes, then add in chopped vegetarian pepperoni and remove from heat.

3. Spread goat cheese on bottom half of each dough round and add mushroom mixture. Fold the top half of each dough round over the bottom to make calzones. Crimp shut with a fork.

4. Bake calzones in a covered grill until sizzling and golden brown, about 8–10 minutes.

Italian Caponata Pizza

Serves 4

4 ounces cornmeal

1¼ pounds pizza dough

¼ cup flavored olive oil

1 medium eggplant, peeled and cut into small cubes

1 medium zucchini, diced

½ small red onion, peeled and chopped

½ cup Sicilian green olives, pitted and chopped

¼ cup small capers

Salt and pepper to taste

1 cup tomato sauce

8 ounces mozzarella cheese, shredded

4 ounces Parmesan cheese, grated

Be sure to use low or indirect heat when grilling pizza to avoid an overly crisp crust. Covering the grill helps distribute the heat evenly.

1. Sprinkle the cornmeal on a flat work surface and roll out the dough.

2. Heat the olive oil on the stovetop, and add the eggplant, zucchini, onion, olives, capers, salt, and pepper. Sauté until the onion is soft. Add the tomato sauce.

3. Spread the sauced vegetables on the dough. Sprinkle with mozzarella and then with Parmesan.

4. Place pizza on the grill and heat, covered, for about 7 minutes, or until done.

Magical, Meltable Mozzarella

Like most good things, the richer the cheese, the smoother and tastier. Low-fat mozzarella tastes like nothing and acts like chewing gum. If you can find it, try imported buffalo's milk mozzarella—it's delectably creamy and melts beautifully. It's worth the extra calories and money it costs.

Apple Cider "Sausages"

Serves 8

1½ cups apple cider
1 cup apple cider vinegar
8 store-bought vegetarian sausages

Some people find the taste of store-bought vegetarian sausages a bit bland. This apple cider simmering method fixes that right up. Add apple chunks and turn them into skewers.

1. Put cider and cider vinegar in a large saucepan. Prick the sausages with a fork and place them in the cider-and-vinegar mix. Bring to a simmer and cook on low for 30 minutes.

2. Allow sausages to cool in the cider mixture.

3. Grill until lightly browned, following package instructions.

Garlic Portobellos in Beurre Blanc

Serves 4

1 pound portobello mushrooms

3 cloves garlic, sliced thin

¼ cup olive oil

¼ cup balsamic vinegar

1½ cups vegetable stock

½ cup white wine

2 tablespoons butter

Chopped fresh parsley (optional)

Earthy mushrooms pair with a simple white-wine-and-butter sauce. Turn it into a fuller meal by slicing the grilled mushrooms and serving them atop small shell pasta, gnocchi, or fluffed orzo.

1. Wash mushrooms and remove stems. Place mushrooms flat in a glass baking dish and set aside.

2. In a saucepan over low heat, sauté the garlic cloves in olive oil. Remove garlic cloves and stir in vinegar. Pour this over the mushrooms to coat. Marinate 20 minutes, turning once.

3. Grill mushrooms about 6 minutes (3 minutes per side).

4. Heat stock and wine in a saucepan until it simmers. Simmer 10 minutes. Whisk in butter. To serve, plate mushrooms and drizzle generously with warm sauce. Garnish with parsley if desired.

Mixed Tikka Masala Kebabs

Serves 4

5 small fingerling or new potatoes, halved or quartered

Water for boiling

16 1" chunks tofu, seitan, or store-bought chicken substitute

12 button mushrooms

12 pearl onions (or regular onions, chopped into chunks)

1 cup plain or soy yogurt

1 tablespoon lemon juice

3 cloves garlic, minced

2 teaspoons fresh ginger, minced

2 teaspoons paprika

1 teaspoon curry powder

1 teaspoon chili powder

1 teaspoon turmeric

½ teaspoon cumin

½ teaspoon sugar

¼ teaspoon salt

Don't skimp on the marinating time here—and double it if you can. Serve with Cardamom Naan (see recipe in Chapter 2).

1. Simmer potatoes in water for 3–4 minutes until barely tender; do not overcook. Allow to cool. Place potatoes, tofu, mushrooms, and onions in a large shallow container.

2. In a separate small bowl, combine the remaining ingredients, then pour over potato-and-tofu mix, coating well.

3. Allow ingredients to marinate for at least 1 hour (2–3 is better), then place on skewers.

4. Place skewers on a well-greased grill for 8–10 minutes, turning once or twice and basting with extra marinade sauce.

Chapter 10

Grilled Fruits and Desserts

California Grilled Figs with White Wine Sauce

Serves 4

¼ cup white wine
2 tablespoons maple syrup
2 teaspoons Dijon mustard
1 tablespoon olive oil
4 fresh figs, sliced in half
Salt and pepper to taste

Serve gently grilled figs as a light side dish, or add to a green salad with crumbled blue cheese. California figs go with any chilled Moscato wine or a California Sauvignon Blanc.

1. Simmer white wine, maple syrup, and Dijon mustard over low heat, for 3–4 minutes, until combined and slightly reduced. Remove from heat and add olive oil.

2. Baste figs and season lightly with salt and pepper.

3. Grill figs for 5–7 minutes, basting frequently and turning once or twice. Do not overcook. Figs should still hold their shape when done.

Chocolate Cheese Martabak Waffles

Serves 2

2 large frozen waffles, thawed

2 tablespoons butter or margarine

3 tablespoons mini chocolate chips or chocolate sprinkles

3 tablespoons grated white Cheddar cheese

This gooey waffle sandwich was inspired by martabak, *a popular streetside snack in the Indonesian city of Padang. Vendors there boast an array of various toppings to fill these doughy sandwiches, but most tourists come to love the sweet-and-savory combination of chocolate and cheese.*

1. Spread each waffle with 1 tablespoon of butter. Place 1 waffle, butter-side down, on a large square of aluminum foil.

2. Sprinkle the waffle with a layer of chocolate chips, and then a layer of cheese, and place the second waffle on top, butter-side up, to form a sandwich, gently pressing the two waffles together.

3. Wrap in foil and place over medium-low or indirect heat for 8–10 minutes, turning once.

Butter-Basted Apples with Walnuts and Softened Roquefort

Serves 3

2 large apples, cored
3 tablespoons butter, melted
¼ cup chopped walnuts
¼ cup crumbled Roquefort or other blue cheese, at room temperature
Honey or agave nectar to taste (optional)

Though inspired by traditional French Roquefort salad, this recipe would work fine with any blue cheese. Blue cheeses pair best with a French Sauternes but a Sauvignon Blanc would also complement the flavors. Or pair these apples with a sweet Port if you're serving them as part of a dessert course.

1. Slice apples into rings and baste with melted butter. Grill for 8–10 minutes, turning once or twice, until a bit soft.

2. Remove from grill and plate immediately, topping each ring with a bit of blue cheese and chopped walnuts.

3. Drizzle with honey, if desired.

Wine Pairing 101

Two philosophies have long ruled the art of the sommelier when it comes to pairing food and wine. One method is to match the flavors: earthy wines, such as a Pinot noir, with an earthy dish, such as portobellos. The other method is to complement the flavors: pair a spicy meal with a sweet wine, for example. Traditional pairing rules dictate that lighter foods, such as salads and vegetable dishes, go better with lighter wines and white wines, while heartier fare, such as burgers and seitan, go better with reds. For hot days and backyard gatherings, stay away from heavy wines such as Cabernet Sauvignon and Syrah, but don't shy away from rosés and sparkling wines, which pair well with a variety of foods, particularly appetizers. Regional pairings can be fun—try a Tuscan dish with a Tuscan red—but don't assume that this is always the best choice. The bottom line? Choose wines that you like. No sense picking out a vintage Pinot grigio if you're a red wine aficionado.

Honey Rum Grapefruit Flambé

Serves 4

2 large grapefruit
¼ cup honey
4 teaspoons unsalted butter
¼ cup golden rum

There's absolutely no rule that says you can't grill for breakfast or brunch, and this is a simple yet exquisite recipe to add to the morning menu.

1. Arrange a large piece of heavy-duty aluminum foil on the grill. Spray foil with nonstick spray and prepare grill for low heat.

2. Cut the grapefruit in half and place on the foil, cut-side down. Close the lid and heat for 3–4 minutes.

3. Turn the grapefruit over and drizzle with honey. Close lid and heat for 3 more minutes, then transfer to a flame-proof platter.

4. Run a knife around the grapefruit sections without cutting through the skin. Dot with butter, and drizzle with rum. Light with a match and serve flaming.

Grilled Peaches with Sweetened Balsamic Reduction

Serves 3

½ cup balsamic vinegar
2 teaspoons brown sugar
3 peaches, sliced in half, pit removed

Pair these grilled peaches with ice cream, or sprinkle with candied pecans for a dairy-free dessert. The balsamic sauce pairs with a variety of summer fruits, not just peaches. Try it with grilled figs, nectarines, or even grapefruit.

1. Simmer vinegar and brown sugar over low heat until reduced to a little less than ¼ cup, about 3–5 minutes, stirring constantly. Remove from heat immediately.

2. Place peaches on a well-greased grill, cut-side down. Grill for 5–6 minutes until soft. Plate, and drizzle generously with balsamic sauce.

Fruit Liqueur Skewers

Serves 2

¼ cup fruit-flavored liqueur, such as Grand Marnier

¼ cup brown sugar

20 1" cubes honeydew, watermelon, or cantaloupe (or a combination)

Serve these skewers with a dollop of Greek yogurt or sweetened mascarpone or put them on top of fruit sorbets. For a primal experience, just eat them off the stick. For a nicer presentation, use a melon baller to create spheres rather than chopped cubes. The fruit is just a suggestion; use any kind you like.

1. Combine liqueur and brown sugar, whisking firmly to dissolve sugar, and marinate fruit for at least 20 minutes.

2. Arrange fruit on skewers and place on a well-greased grill for about 10 minutes, turning several times and basting with extra sauce.

Watch Out for Flare-Ups!

Anytime you're using alcohol on the grill, there's a chance it will flame, especially when you're basting ingredients that are already on the grill. Most flare-ups are small and add to the grilling experience, but be sure to be careful when brushing on extra sauce, especially if you're fond of having eyebrows and don't particularly want them singed off.

Peanut Butter Banana Smoosh

Serves 4

4 ripe bananas

¼–½ cup peanut butter chips, or a combination of peanut butter chips and chocolate chips

These bananas are messy, smooshy, gooey, and absolutely heavenly.

1. Starting in the middle of each unpeeled banana, slice the banana lengthwise first in one direction and then the other, leaving about ¼" unsliced at either end and leaving the bottom of the peel intact. Do not peel.

2. Mash the banana slightly, and stuff as many peanut butter chips as you can fit inside the banana peel.

3. Grill over low or indirect heat away from coals for about 8 minutes.

Chocolate-Filled Peaches

Serves 3

3 large peaches, sliced in half, pits removed

Softened butter or margarine, for brushing

½ cup chocolate chips

Whipped cream

This is an absolutely fool-proof recipe. Just grill up some peaches, fill them with chocolate, and heat till the whole thing is soft and gooey and delicious.

1. Lightly brush peaches with butter. Place on grill, cut-side down, over high heat for 1–2 minutes, then flip over.

2. Sprinkle center of peaches with chocolate chips, and keep on the grill just until chocolate has melted. Top with a generous dollop of whipped cream.

Apricots and Pecans en Papillote

Serves 4

2 tablespoons brown sugar

2 tablespoons vegan margarine, melted

1 tablespoon maple syrup

¼ teaspoon cinnamon or nutmeg

⅓ cup chopped candied pecans

8 apricots, sliced

When the little packets are filled with such a lovely filling and not just odds and ends, the French term "en papillote" sounds much more appropriate than the usual slangy "hobo packets."

1. In a small bowl, combine the brown sugar and melted margarine until creamy and well mixed. Add maple syrup and cinnamon, then add chopped pecans.

2. Place two apricot halves on a sheet of foil, then top each half with pecan mixture. Wrap tightly and place on the grill over medium to low heat for 10–12 minutes, or until apricots are tender.

Grilled Peach Cinnamon Crisp

Serves 4

½ cup oatmeal

3 tablespoons candied ginger, finely chopped (optional)

¼ cup brown sugar

2 tablespoons flour

1½ teaspoons cinnamon

½ teaspoon nutmeg

¼ cup vegan margarine, cold

4 peaches, sliced

Serve with ice cream and crumbled gingersnap cookies on top.

1. Combine oatmeal, ginger, brown sugar, flour, cinnamon, and nutmeg in a bowl, then cut in cold margarine until well mixed and crumbly.

2. Divide peaches into 4 lightly greased foil sheets and top with oatmeal mixture.

3. Fold foil and close tightly to make packets. Grill over low heat, covered, until peaches are tender, about 15 minutes.

Graham Cracker Sandwiches

Serves 4

4 graham crackers, broken in half

2 1.55-ounce (43 grams) chocolate bars, broken in half

Unwrapping these foil packets feels just as exciting as Christmas day—you know there's something good in there and you just can't wait to get at it! You'll probably want to eat more than one, so plan on a double batch. Use a vegan dark chocolate to make them vegan. If you can't find vegan chocolate bars, vegan chocolate chips would work well too. Use lots!

1. Place ½ a bar of chocolate on ½ a graham cracker, then place the other ½ of the graham cracker on top to form a sandwich.
2. Wrap each sandwich tightly in foil individually and place over medium heat on the grill for 3–4 minutes.

Try It With . . .

If you're lucky enough to have a source of gelatin-free marshmallows, by all means, use this recipe to make foil-wrapped S'mores. Otherwise, for variety, try spreading a little bit of peanut butter on the graham crackers, or try it with strawberry or raspberry jam. What the heck, add both!

Grilled Nectarines with Vanilla Whipped Cream

Serves 4

½ cup heavy cream

2 tablespoons sugar

½ teaspoon vanilla

4 firm nectarines, halved and pitted

2 tablespoons slivered almonds, toasted

Try chopped pecans or macadamias in lieu of the almonds, if you prefer. For presentation at a formal gathering, add a bit of sliced cinnamon stick on top of each cream-topped nectarine.

1. Whip the cream, gradually adding the sugar and vanilla. Set aside.

2. Over low heat, grill the nectarines for 1 minute on the cut side, turn over, then grill for another 30 seconds.

3. To serve, plate the nectarines and fill the center with cream, garnishing each with almonds.

Caribbean Cloved Pineapple Skewers

Serves 4

4 teaspoons brown sugar or regular white sugar

1 teaspoon ground cloves

1 teaspoon lemon juice

16 chunks fresh pineapple

Ground cloves add a spicy Caribbean flavor to sweetened grilled pineapple.

1. Mix sugar, cloves, and lemon juice in a bowl. Thread the pineapple onto the skewers and sprinkle with sugar mixture.

2. Grill pineapple over hot fire until slightly browned and very hot. Serve immediately.

Grill-Baked Cranberry Pear Crisp

Serves 4

2 apples, peeled, cored, and chopped

2 pears, peeled, cored, and chopped

½ cup fresh cranberries, stems removed

2 tablespoons flour

1 teaspoon grated orange zest

1 cup brown sugar, divided

½ teaspoon salt

1 tablespoon lemon juice

½ teaspoon ground cinnamon

½ teaspoon allspice

¼ teaspoon nutmeg

¼ cup plus 2 tablespoons butter or margarine, divided

⅔ cup oatmeal

This colorful apple and pear crisp is filled with all the flavors of fall, including fresh cranberries, nutmeg, and allspice. Try it for brunch.

1. Prepare a heavy cast-iron skillet with nonstick spray.

2. Mix the apples, pears, and cranberries with flour, orange zest, ½ cup brown sugar, salt, lemon juice, cinnamon, allspice, and nutmeg. Put fruit in the prepared skillet and dot with 2 tablespoons cold butter.

3. Melt ¼ cup butter. Mix the remaining ½ cup brown sugar, oatmeal, and melted butter together and spread over the fruit.

4. Place skillet directly on the grill over low or indirect heat. Cover, and heat for 20 minutes or until topping is crisp and the fruit bubbling.

Melting Banana Splits

Serves 4

4 bananas, sliced in half lengthwise

4 scoops vanilla, strawberry, or chocolate ice cream

¼–½ cup chocolate sauce, heated

½ cup walnuts, chopped

Remember the good ol' days when you could share a banana split with a friend at the drugstore soda fountain for a quarter? Neither do I, but I hear it was nice. Use dairy-free ice cream and chocolate sauce to keep it vegan, or top it off with whipped cream and maraschino cherries.

1. Place bananas on the grill over low heat. Grill for just 1–2 minutes on each side.

2. Arrange bananas on serving dish and scoop ice cream on top. Top with chocolate sauce and walnuts and eat immediately.

Grilling Bananas

Try flaming your grilled bananas with a fruit liqueur, Limoncello, or a fruity tropical rum. All of the alcohol cooks away, leaving a delightful flavor. For kids, melt a bit of jam to brush on bananas while they're on the grill.

Strawberry Kiwi Cake Kebabs with Minted Yogurt

Serves 4

3 teaspoons lemon juice

2 tablespoons brown sugar

2 tablespoons butter or margarine

12 fresh strawberries

4 kiwis, chopped into fourths

½ store-bought angel food cake, chopped into 20 1" cubes

1 8-ounce container plain or lemon-flavored yogurt or soy yogurt

3 tablespoons chopped fresh mint

Pound cake works on the grill, as does angel food cake, but a sweet brioche, challah, or even a Hawaiian loaf bread could be substituted.

1. Whisk together the lemon juice, brown sugar, and butter. Skewer strawberries, kiwis, and cake onto skewers and brush with butter mixture.

2. Place skewers on the grill over low heat, and grill for 1–2 minutes on each side.

3. Combine yogurt and mint and serve with fruit-and-cake kebabs as a dipping sauce.

Smoky Applesauce

Serves 4

4 large apples

2 tablespoons vegan margarine

½–⅔ cup apple cider

¼ teaspoon cinnamon

⅛ teaspoon nutmeg

2 teaspoons brown sugar

½ teaspoon salt

Juice of ½ lemon

Grated zest from ½ lemon

The fiery flavor of the grill really adds to the dish. Who needs liquid smoke when you've got the real thing? Use some fruity wood chips on the coals to bring out even more of a smoky flavor.

1. Peel and core apples, then slice in half. Place on the grill over a hot fire for 1 minute per side.

2. Put the rest of the ingredients in a saucepan and heat. Add the grilled apples to the sauce. If the applesauce is too dry, add more cider.

3. Mix, breaking the apples up with a fork, and heat until thickened. Serve hot, cold, or at room temperature.

Strawberry Rum Shortcake with Honeyed Mascarpone

Serves 6

2 tablespoons brown sugar

¼ cup, plus 1 tablespoon rum, divided

18 strawberries, halved

1 store-bought pound cake

8 ounces mascarpone, room temperature

¼ cup honey

2 tablespoons lemon juice

I may not be old enough to remember soda fountains but I certainly remember Strawberry Shortcake, the children's cartoon character who was my idol for much of the early '80s. But never mind that; this dish is for adults. It'd look lovely served in tall martini glasses, and the honey-rum mascarpone can be prepared in advance.

1. Whisk together brown sugar and ¼ cup rum, and marinate strawberries for at least 1 hour. Skewer, then grill, basting (carefully!) with extra sugar mixture for 3–4 minutes, just until strawberries are gently softened.

2. Slice the pound cake into 1"-thick slices and brush with extra sugar and rum mixture. Place on the grill for just 1–2 minutes on each side, until marked and heated.

3. Beat together the mascarpone with honey, lemon juice, and 1 tablespoon of rum until well combined.

4. To serve, plate slices of pound cake and top with strawberries and a generous dollop of mascarpone.

Changing It Up

As with the Strawberry Kiwi Cake Kebabs with Minted Yogurt (see recipe in this chapter), angel food cake also works well in this recipe. Although the rum-basted strawberries are lovely with a grown-up honey-rum mascarpone, vanilla ice cream or plain whipped cream can also be used to finish it up. If you're omitting the mascarpone, drizzle your ice cream with a red wine reduction or a bit of Pernod for a dramatic finish. Celebrating the Fourth of July? Add blueberries to make this a tricolored treat.

Coconut-Glazed Pineapple

Serves 4

1 12-ounce can coconut milk

½ cup brown sugar

1 large pineapple, sliced into 1"-thick rounds

1 teaspoon cinnamon

¼ cup toasted coconut flakes or fresh chopped mint (optional)

Fresh pineapple enlivens any backyard cookout. Here, thickly sliced pineapple is coated with a tropical coconut glaze and garnished with coconut flakes or fresh mint for presentation.

1. Warm coconut milk in a saucepan over medium heat. Add brown sugar, stirring to dissolve. Heat for just a few minutes until combined. Remove from heat and allow to cool.

2. Coat pineapple with coconut mixture, sprinkle with a bit of cinnamon, then grill, basting with extra sauce, for 5–6 minutes each side.

3. Drizzle with extra marinade and sprinkle with coconut flakes or chopped mint for garnish, if desired.

Double Chocolate Diet Disaster Sandwich

Serves 2

2 slices bread

Butter or margarine, softened

2 "King Size" (about 2 ounces each) chocolate candy bars, any kind (Snickers, Butterfinger, etc.)

2 tablespoons chocolate hazelnut spread

Please don't ask how many calories are in this recipe. You don't want to know.

1. Brush bread with softened butter. Spread 1 slice of bread with chocolate hazelnut spread. Place two candy bars across the bread, parallel, then top with other slice of bread.

2. Place on grill over low or indirect heat for just 2–3 minutes on each side, or until chocolate has melted.

Walnut Cinnamon-Stuffed Apples

Serves 4

4 large Granny Smith apples

¼ cup brown sugar

1 teaspoon cinnamon

¼ teaspoon ground nutmeg

2 tablespoons walnuts, chopped

4 teaspoons vegan margarine

Baked apples are almost as American as apple pie. Try them on the grill, stuffed with walnuts, cinnamon, and nutmeg, and make these sweet grilled apples a new fall family tradition.

1. Remove the apple cores, making sure not to cut all the way through to the bottom or the stuffing will fall out.

2. Mix the sugar, cinnamon, nutmeg, and walnuts together and fill the apples.

3. Use aluminum foil to make cups or rings to hold the apples steady on the grill. Dot the tops of the filling with margarine.

4. Place the apples on the grill over low or indirect heat. Cover and heat for 20 minutes.

Grilled Pears with Cloved Claret Cream

Serves 4

1 cup claret wine

2 whole cloves

¼ cup sugar (optional)

¼ cup heavy cream

4 unpeeled pears, halved and cored

Red wine and cloves transform homemade whipped cream into a gourmet summer dessert when accompanied by lightly grilled pears.

1. Bring the claret, cloves, and sugar to a boil and reduce to half. Add the cream and keep warm.

2. Grill the pears over high heat for 1 minute, cut-side down. Turn over and grill for another 30 seconds. Remove pears to serving plates, spoon with sauce, and serve immediately.

What Is Claret Wine?

A dark red wine from the Bordeaux region of France, claret is a dry red wine frequently used as a table wine. It's actually a blend of several types of grapes that has been mimicked by vintners worldwide, so these days you can find clarets from California to Australia. Substitute a Cabernet Sauvignon if a Bordeaux is unavailable.

Apricots with Strawberry Wine Sauce

Serves 4

1 pint strawberries
½ cup red wine
½ cup sugar
8 medium fresh apricots
1 tablespoon vegan margarine, melted

This is a very refreshing end to a big meal. The sauce is a cinch to make and the apricots take but a few minutes. Pair this dish with ice cream or top it off with whipped cream. Or both.

1. Purée the strawberries, wine, and sugar in a blender. Strain and then heat on the stovetop over a low flame for 10 minutes.

2. Rinse the apricots and cut them in half, removing the pits. Brush apricots with melted margarine.

3. Place the apricots cut-side down on the grill over medium heat for 1 minute. Turn and grill for another 45–60 seconds.

4. Plate and top with strawberry wine sauce. Serve immediately while still hot.

Caribbean Rum and Ginger Fruit Skewers

Serves 3

¼ cup Caribbean rum

2 tablespoons brown sugar

½ teaspoon vanilla extract

1 banana, cut into 1" chunks

16 chunks fresh pineapple

8 fresh strawberries

¼ teaspoon allspice

½ teaspoon cinnamon

½ teaspoon ginger

Fruit brushed with Caribbean rum and paired with Caribbean spices will have you and your friends talking like pirates. Just about any fruit will work in this recipe, so use whatever you like—kiwi, mango, melon—anything, really.

1. Whisk together the rum, brown sugar, and vanilla until sugar is dissolved. Marinate fruit for at least 30 minutes.

2. In a separate small bowl, combine together the allspice, cinnamon, and ginger.

3. Arrange fruit on skewers, basting with rum mixture. Sprinkle with spice blend, then place on a well-greased grill for 2–3 minutes on each side.

Chapter 11

Off the Grill

Lemon Quinoa Veggie Salad

Serves 4

1½ cups quinoa

4 cups vegetable broth

1 cup frozen mixed veggies, thawed

¼ cup lemon juice

¼ cup olive oil

1 teaspoon garlic powder

½ teaspoon sea salt

¼ teaspoon black pepper

2 tablespoons chopped fresh cilantro or parsley (optional)

If you prefer to use fresh veggies, any kind will do. Steamed broccoli or fresh tomatoes work well. Or just toss in whatever you're grilling.

1. In a large pot, simmer quinoa in vegetable broth for 15–20 minutes, stirring occasionally, until liquid is absorbed and quinoa is cooked. Add mixed veggies and stir to combine.

2. Remove from heat and combine with remaining ingredients. Serve hot or cold.

Maple Baked Beans

Serves 6

3 cups navy or pinto beans
9 cups water
1 onion, chopped
⅔ cup maple syrup
¼ cup barbecue sauce
2 tablespoons molasses
1 tablespoon Dijon mustard
1 tablespoon chili powder
1 teaspoon paprika
1½ teaspoons salt
¾ teaspoon pepper

Tailor these saucy Boston-style baked beans to your liking by adding extra molasses, a bit of cayenne, or some TVP crumbles for a meaty texture.

1. Cover beans in water and allow to soak at least 8 hours or overnight.

2. Preheat oven to 350°F.

3. In a large Dutch oven or sturdy stockpot, combine beans and remaining ingredients. Bring to a rolling boil on the stovetop.

4. Cover the pot and transfer to preheated oven. Bake beans in oven for 1½ hours, stirring once or twice. Uncover and cook 1 more hour.

5. Alternatively, beans can be simmered over low heat for 1½–2 hours on the stovetop.

Lemon Mint New Potato Salad

Serves 4

10–12 small new potatoes, chopped	*This is a cooling potato salad for hot days, with yogurt instead of the usual mayonnaise. Use vegan soy yogurt to make it suitable for vegans, and prepare it in advance to allow time for the flavors to fully develop.*

10–12 small new potatoes, chopped

4 cloves garlic, minced

1 tablespoon olive oil

¼ cup chopped mint

2 teaspoons lemon juice

¼ cup yogurt

½ cup green peas

½ red onion, diced (or 2 stalks celery)

Salt and pepper to taste

This is a cooling potato salad for hot days, with yogurt instead of the usual mayonnaise. Use vegan soy yogurt to make it suitable for vegans, and prepare it in advance to allow time for the flavors to fully develop.

1. Preheat oven to 350°F. Line or lightly grease a baking sheet.

2. In a large bowl, toss together the potatoes with the garlic, olive oil, and mint, coating potatoes well.

3. Arrange potatoes on a single layer on baking sheet. Roast for 45 minutes.

4. Whisk together lemon juice and yogurt, and coat potatoes well with mixture. Gently toss with green peas and red onions. Season with salt and pepper just before serving.

Tempeh "Chicken" Salad

Serves 3

1 8-ounce package tempeh, diced small

Water for boiling

3 tablespoons vegan mayonnaise

2 teaspoons lemon juice

½ teaspoon garlic powder

1 teaspoon Dijon mustard

2 tablespoons sweet pickle relish

½ cup green peas

2 stalks celery, diced small

1 tablespoon chopped fresh dill (optional)

Turn it into a sandwich, or slice up some tomatoes and serve on a bed of lettuce.

1. Cover tempeh with water and simmer for 10 minutes, until tempeh is soft. Drain and allow to cool completely.

2. Whisk together mayonnaise, lemon juice, garlic powder, mustard, and relish.

3. Combine tempeh, mayonnaise mixture, peas, celery, and dill and gently toss to combine.

4. Chill for at least 1 hour before serving to allow flavors to combine. If desired, serve as a sandwich filling in a roll or between two slices of bread.

Curried Chicken Tempeh

For curried chicken salad, omit the dill and add ½ teaspoon curry powder and a dash cayenne and black pepper. If you don't feel up to dicing and simmering tempeh, try combining the dressing with store-bought mock chicken, or even veggie turkey or deli slices.

All-American Classic Potato Salad

Serves 10

1 teaspoon salt

2½ pounds small red potatoes, unpeeled

3 stalks celery, sliced

½ red onion, minced

½ cup plain yogurt

½ cup mayonnaise

2 green onions, with tops, finely chopped

¼ cup fresh parsley, chopped, plus additional for garnish

1 teaspoon dry mustard

¼ teaspoon salt

⅛ teaspoon freshly ground pepper

For a perfect potato salad, simmer the potatoes until just barely soft, then drain and immediately rinse under cold water to stop them from cooking further and getting too soft. You don't want a mushy potato salad!

1. Fill a large pot with water, allowing room for potatoes, and bring to boil. Add the salt and potatoes. Boil about 20 minutes, or until tender but not mushy. Drain and allow to cool. Cut the unpeeled potatoes into ½" cubes.

2. In a large bowl, combine potatoes, celery, and red onion. Toss gently to mix. In a small bowl, whisk together the yogurt, mayonnaise, green onions, parsley, mustard, salt, and pepper. Pour the dressing over the potato mixture. Using a large spoon, mix gently to avoid mashing the potatoes. Cover and chill at least 2 hours before serving. Garnish with fresh parsley.

Texas Caviar

Serves 8

2 ripe, firm avocados

2 tablespoons vegetable oil

3 tablespoons Tabasco sauce

2 tablespoons red wine vinegar

1 teaspoon coarse ground black pepper

1 bulb fresh garlic, minced

1 15-ounce can of whole kernel corn, drained and rinsed

1 15-ounce can of black-eyed peas, drained and rinsed

1 15-ounce can of black beans, drained and rinsed

1 bunch of fresh cilantro, chopped

2 medium-size tomatoes, cubed

1 small red onion, chopped

It may be a favorite in Texas, but this tangy salad was actually first invented by a native of New York City in the 1950s. Sorry, Texans!

1. Cut avocados into ½" cubes. In a small bowl, mix together vegetable oil, Tabasco sauce, vinegar, pepper, and garlic. Pour mixture over avocados and stir gently to coat.

2. In large bowl, mix corn, peas, beans, cilantro, tomatoes, and onion. Add avocado mixture to large bowl and gently mix with other ingredients. Serve as a salad or with tortilla chips or crackers.

Wild Rice Salad with Apples and Almonds

Serves 8

½ cup wild rice

Salted water for simmering

½ cup shelled almonds, whole or in slivers

1 tablespoon oil

1 large onion, roughly chopped

1 Rome or Golden Delicious apple, peeled, cored, and diced

¼ cup raisins

Salt and freshly ground black pepper to taste

1 tablespoon olive oil

¼ cup chopped cilantro or parsley

Wild rice is not actually rice, but rather a seed. With almost 7 grams of protein per cup when cooked, wild rice is an excellent source of protein.

1. Boil the rice in 2½ quarts salted water until tender, about 40 minutes; drain, reserving cooking liquid.

2. Crisp the almonds by toasting them dry until fragrant for just 1–2 minutes (optional).

3. Heat the oil in a large skillet or Dutch oven over medium heat for 1 minute. Add onion; cook until softened, about 5 minutes. Add the apples, raisins, and a splash of the water reserved from cooking the rice. Cook 5 minutes more, until the apples are translucent.

4. Combine the cooked rice, the apple mixture, the toasted almonds, and salt and pepper. Stir in olive oil and serve garnished with cilantro or parsley.

Lemon Thyme Orzo with Asparagus

Serves 4

1½ cups orzo

1 bunch asparagus, chopped

2 tablespoons olive oil

Zest from 1 lemon

2 tablespoons lemon juice

½ teaspoon salt

¼ teaspoon pepper

2 teaspoons chopped fresh thyme

The combination of lemon and thyme is understated and rustic; it smells and tastes terrific. If asparagus isn't in season, use green peas or lightly steamed broccoli.

1. Cook orzo according to package instructions.

2. In a large skillet, heat asparagus in olive oil until just tender. Do not overcook.

3. Reduce heat to low and add in orzo and remaining ingredients, stirring to combine. Cook for just 1–2 minutes, until heated through, and adjust seasonings to taste.

What Is Orzo?

Despite its abundant use at gourmet eateries, there's really nothing fancy about orzo: it's just a funny sounding word for "small rice-shaped pasta." In other words, it's just pasta. Because of its small size, it can be used more like couscous and rice than other pastas, and works with lighter and thinner sauces and in pilaf-like salads.

Southeast Asian Slaw

Serves 4

¼ head (about ½ pound) napa cabbage

½ carrot, grated

1 small red onion, julienned

1 small red Thai chili or jalapeño pepper, finely chopped

¼ cup chopped cilantro

Juice of 1 lime

1 tablespoon rice wine vinegar

1 teaspoon sugar

1 teaspoon vegetable oil

A few drops sesame oil

½ teaspoon salt

Plate this Thai-fusion salad with Vietnamese Lemongrass Tofu (see Chapter 7) or the Easy Sweet Indonesian Seitan Satay (see Chapter 8) for a culinary tour of the Asian tropics.

1. Shred the cabbage as fine as you possibly can, using a knife or mandoline. Combine with carrot, onion, chili pepper, and cilantro.

2. Whisk together the lime juice, rice wine vinegar, sugar, vegetable oil, sesame oil, and salt, then toss thoroughly with cabbage mixture.

3. Refrigerate for at least 30 minutes before serving.

Sweet White Salad with Shaved Asiago

Serves 4

4 ounces (about 2 heads) frisée or fine curly endive

4 heads Belgian endive, cut into 1" pieces

1 cup julienne of jicama

1 small sweet onion, sliced into paper-thin rings

Juice of ½ lemon (about 2 tablespoons)

1 tablespoon olive oil

1 teaspoon orange juice concentrate

Salt and pepper to taste

Asiago cheese for shaving

Frisée (curly lettuce) and endive combine with jicama and white cheese for a fresh and crunchy summer salad. Romano or even Parmesan can be used in place of the Asiago, if you prefer.

1. Wash and dry the frisée and combine with Belgian endive, jicama, and onions. Whisk together the lemon juice, olive oil, orange juice concentrate, salt, and pepper; toss with salad to coat.

2. Arrange salad onto 4 plates, piling it as high as possible. Using a peeler, gently shave several curls of Asiago cheese over each salad, and serve immediately.

Succotash Corn Salad

Serves 8

8 ears sweet corn, shucked (or 16 ounces frozen corn)

½ pound dried pinto or red kidney beans, cooked or 2 16-ounce cans, drained and rinsed

¼ cup champagne vinegar or rice wine vinegar

¼ cup olive oil

¼ cup chives, chopped

Salt and pepper to taste

In New England, fresh cranberry beans are in the market in June and July, and they are delicious in this high-protein salad combined with fresh summer sweet corn.

1. Shave corn kernels from cob, shearing them from the stem end to the tip with a knife. Cook in rapidly boiling salted water for 1 minute.

2. Toss with beans, vinegar, oil, and chives; season with salt and pepper to taste.

Five-Minute Vegan Pasta Salad

Serves 4

4 cups cooked pasta, cooled

¾ cup vegan Italian salad dressing

3 scallions, chopped

½ cup sliced black olives

1 tomato, chopped

1 avocado, diced (optional)

Salt and pepper to taste

Once you've got the pasta cooked and cooled, this takes just 5 minutes to assemble, as it's made with store-bought dressing. A balsamic vinaigrette or tomato dressing also works.

1. Toss together all ingredients. Allow to chill for at least 1½ hours before serving, if time allows, to allow flavors to combine.

Easy Three-Bean Salad

Serves 6

1 16-ounce can green beans, drained

1 16-ounce can yellow wax beans, drained

1 16-ounce can red kidney beans, drained

1 onion

½ cup sugar

⅔ cup vinegar

⅓ cup vegetable oil

½ teaspoon salt

⅛ teaspoon pepper

Almost as popular as potato salad and coleslaw at summer gatherings is a mixed bean salad. This is an old-fashioned recipe, with just oil, vinegar, and sugar to dress the beans.

1. Drain the beans. Slice the onion thinly, then cut the slices into quarters. Whisk together the sugar, vinegar, oil, salt, and pepper. Combine the beans, onions, and dressing, mixing.

2. Chill at least 4 hours, or overnight, stirring occasionally. If desired, salad can be drained before serving.

Orange Fruit Salad

Serves 4

3 cups roasted cubed butternut squash

2 carrots, shredded

2 cups fresh papaya, diced

2 tablespoons fresh ginger, minced

Juice of 1 lime

2 tablespoons plain or soy yogurt

1 tablespoon honey or agave nectar

1 tablespoon olive oil

Salt and fresh ground black pepper

Grill extra butternut squash to make this orange salad, or just roast a bit of the frozen packaged kind in the oven with a bit of olive oil.

1. Combine the squash, carrots, and papaya in a large salad bowl. Set aside.

2. Stir together the ginger, lime juice, yogurt, honey, olive oil, salt, and pepper until well combined. Toss the dressing with the salad ingredients and serve chilled.

German Potato Salad

Serves 5

1 pound Red Bliss, fingerling, or new potatoes

Cold water for simmering

1 tablespoon salt

½ cup red wine vinegar

¾ cup olive oil

1 red onion, peeled and sliced paper thin

1 teaspoon peppercorns, cracked

1 teaspoon caraway seeds, cracked

½ cup fresh parsley, rinsed and chopped

Garnish this tangy German-style potato salad with a few chopped scallions or vegetarian bacon bits. Or, for a pink potato salad, add leftover roasted and sliced beets.

1. Scrub the potatoes but do not peel. Cut into bite-sized pieces. Put them in cold water with salt and bring to a boil. Boil potatoes for about 20 minutes, depending on size, until soft.

2. While the potatoes are cooking, mix the rest of the ingredients in a large serving bowl to make the dressing.

3. Drain the potatoes and mix them with the dressing. Serve hot, cold, or at room temperature.

Louisiana Coleslaw

Serves 6

1 pound cabbage, shredded (about 4 cups)

1 green bell pepper, diced small

1 carrot, grated

1 medium onion, diced small

1 cup mayonnaise or vegan mayonnaise

3 tablespoons apple cider vinegar

2 tablespoons Dijon mustard

3 tablespoons sweet relish

1 tablespoon Creole spice blend

1 teaspoon hot sauce (or to taste)

2 teaspoons minced fresh cayenne or jalapeño pepper (optional)

Salt and pepper to taste

Use a Louisiana hot sauce to bring home a touch of the South, no matter where you live. As a side dish, chilled coleslaw goes with grilled seitan, tempeh, or burgers, or use it as a condiment to top off sandwiches or veggie dogs.

1. Combine the shredded cabbage, bell pepper, carrot, and onion in a large bowl.

2. In a separate small bowl, whisk together the mayonnaise, cider vinegar, and mustard until combined, then stir in the sweet relish, Creole spice blend, hot sauce, and cayenne pepper. Combine with cabbage mixture, tossing to coat cabbage.

3. Chill at least 1 hour before serving to let the flavors blend. Toss again just before serving, season with salt and pepper, and adjust seasonings to taste.

Spices of the South

Can't find a Creole spice blend? Make your own! Combine 1 heaping tablespoon of sweet paprika with 1 teaspoon each of onion powder, garlic powder, oregano, and thyme. Add ½ teaspoon of salt and ¼ teaspoon of pepper. Give it a bit of a kick by adding in ¼–½ teaspoon cayenne pepper, depending on how hot you like it.

Black Bean and Butternut Squash Chili

Serves 4

1 onion, chopped

3 cloves garlic, minced

2 tablespoons oil

1 medium butternut squash, chopped into chunks

2 15-ounce cans black beans, drained

1 28-ounce can stewed or diced tomatoes, undrained

¾ cup water or vegetable broth

1 tablespoon chili powder

1 teaspoon cumin

¼ teaspoon cayenne pepper, or to taste

½ teaspoon salt

2 tablespoons chopped fresh cilantro (optional)

The sweetness of the butternut squash complements the spicy Southwestern flavors in this Tex-Mex chili, but another squash, such as pumpkin or even sweet potatoes, could be substituted.

1. In a large stockpot, sauté onion and garlic in oil until soft, about 4 minutes.

2. Reduce heat and add remaining ingredients, except cilantro.

3. Cover and simmer for 25 minutes. Uncover and simmer another five minutes. Top with fresh cilantro just before serving.

Carrot and Date Salad

Serves 4

⅓ cup tahini

1 tablespoon olive oil

2 tablespoons agave nectar (or 2 teaspoons sugar)

3 tablespoons lemon juice

¼ teaspoon salt

4 large carrots, grated

½ cup chopped dates

3 Satsuma or mandarin oranges, sectioned

⅓ cup coconut flakes (optional)

If you're used to carrot and raisin salads with pineapple and drowning in mayonnaise, this lighter and healthier version with tahini, dates, and mandarin oranges will be a welcome change.

1. In a small bowl, whisk together the tahini, olive oil, agave nectar, lemon juice, and salt.

2. Place grated carrots in a large bowl, and toss with tahini mixture. Add dates, oranges, and coconut flakes and combine.

3. Allow to sit for at least 1 hour before serving, to soften carrots and dates. Toss again before serving.

Deli-Style Macaroni Salad

Serves 6

3 cups cooked macaroni

1 carrot, diced small

½ cup green peas

½ cup corn

1 rib celery, diced

½ cup mayonnaise

1½ tablespoons prepared mustard

2 tablespoons white or apple cider vinegar

2 teaspoons sugar

2 tablespoons pickle relish

1 tablespoon chopped fresh dill (optional)

Salt and pepper to taste

Add a can of kidney beans or chickpeas to turn this classic creamy salad into a protein-rich main dish, and use vegan mayonnaise to make it vegan.

1. Combine the macaroni, carrot, peas, corn, and celery in a large bowl.

2. In a separate small bowl, whisk together the mayonnaise, mustard, vinegar, sugar, and relish, and combine with macaroni.

3. Stir in the fresh dill and season with salt and pepper to taste.

4. Chill for at least 2 hours before serving, to allow flavors to combine and to soften veggies.

Pasta Salad Secrets

One secret to making flavorful vegan pasta salads is to use heavily salted water when boiling the pasta. So go ahead, dump in 1 full tablespoon (or even 2!) of salt to the cooking water.

Easy Creamy Coleslaw

Serves 6

1 medium head cabbage

¼ cup cider vinegar

¼ cup mayonnaise

2 tablespoons half-and-half (or cream)

1 tablespoon sugar

1 small sweet gherkin, diced (optional)

1½ teaspoons black pepper

1 teaspoon salt

The history of coleslaw in America goes all the way back to the earliest Dutch settlers of New Amsterdam who dressed shredded cabbage grown along the Hudson River in oil, vinegar, salt, and pepper. Mayonnaise didn't come along until later.

1. Finely chop cabbage (or coarsely grate if you prefer) and place in a large bowl.

2. Mix together the vinegar, mayonnaise, half-and-half, sugar, gherkin, pepper, and salt. Pour over cabbage and toss. Refrigerate for at least 1 hour before serving.

California Picnic Pasta Salad

Serves 6

3 cups cooked corkscrew or bow-tie pasta

2 large tomatoes, diced

½ cup jarred banana peppers, sliced thin

½ red onion, diced

½ cup sliced black olives

2 tablespoons olive oil

1 tablespoon lemon juice

2 teaspoons Dijon mustard

1 tablespoon red wine vinegar

½ teaspoon basil

½ teaspoon oregano

Salt and pepper to taste

2 avocados, diced

Keep the avocados separate until just before serving. To transport, pack diced avocados in a separate container drizzled with just a bit of lemon juice to keep them from browning, and toss them in when it's time to eat.

1. Combine the pasta, tomatoes, peppers, onion, and olives in a large bowl.

2. In a separate small bowl, whisk together the remaining ingredients, except avocado, until well mixed.

3. Chill for at least 1 hour. Add diced avocado and toss gently, then serve immediately.

Instant Add-Ons

Open up a jar and instantly add color, flavor, and texture to a basic pasta salad. What's in your cupboard? Try capers, roasted red peppers, canned veggies, jarred pimentos or sun-dried tomatoes, or even mandarin oranges or sliced beets. Snip in any leftover fresh herbs you have on hand.

No-Mayo Napa Coleslaw

Serves 4

1 head napa cabbage, shredded

1 carrot, grated

2 green onions, chopped

1 red bell pepper, sliced thin

2 tablespoons olive oil

2 tablespoons apple cider vinegar

2 teaspoons soy sauce

½ teaspoon sesame oil

2 tablespoons maple syrup

2 tablespoons sesame seeds (optional)

Napa cabbage, native to northern China, is said to have brought wealth and fertility to the courts of imperial Beijing. Perhaps this recipe will do the same for you.

1. Toss together the cabbage, carrot, green onions, and bell pepper in a large bowl.

2. In a separate small bowl, whisk together the olive oil, vinegar, soy sauce, sesame oil, and maple syrup until combined.

3. Drizzle dressing over cabbage and veggies, add sesame seeds (if desired), and toss to combine.

Sesame Snow Pea Rice Pilaf

Serves 6

4 cups cooked rice

2 tablespoons olive or sunflower oil

1 tablespoon sesame oil

2 tablespoons soy sauce

3 tablespoons apple cider vinegar

1 teaspoon sugar

1 cup snow peas, chopped

¾ cup baby corn, chopped

3 scallions, chopped

2 tablespoons chopped fresh parsley

½ teaspoon sea salt

This Asian-inspired salad keeps, so prepare it in advance, if you need. Sauté some tofu and give the leftovers a quick stir-fry to turn them into fried rice.

1. In a large pot over low heat, combine the rice, olive oil, sesame oil, soy sauce, vinegar, and sugar, stirring to combine.

2. Add snow peas, baby corn, and scallions and heat until warmed through and vegetables are lightly cooked, stirring frequently so the rice doesn't burn.

3. While still hot, stir in fresh parsley and season with sea salt. Chill before serving.

Super Meaty TVP Chili

Serves 6

1½ cups TVP granules

1 cup hot vegetable broth

1 tablespoon soy sauce

1 yellow onion, chopped

5 cloves garlic, minced

2 tablespoons olive oil

1 cup corn kernels (fresh, frozen, or canned)

1 bell pepper, any color, chopped

2 15-ounce cans beans (black, kidney, or pinto)

1 15-ounce can diced tomatoes

1 jalapeño pepper, minced or ½ teaspoon cayenne pepper (optional)

1 teaspoon cumin

2 tablespoons chili powder

Salt and pepper to taste

Any mock meat will work well in a vegetarian chili, but TVP is easy to keep on hand and very inexpensive. This is more of a thick, "meaty" Texas chili than a vegetable chili, but chili is easy and forgiving, so if you want to toss in some zucchini, broccoli, or diced carrots, by all means, do!

1. Cover the TVP with hot vegetable broth and soy sauce and set aside. Allow to sit for 3–4 minutes only, then drain.

2. In a large soup or stock pot, sauté the onion and garlic in olive oil until onions are soft, about 3–4 minutes.

3. Add remaining ingredients and TVP, stirring well to combine. Cover, and allow to simmer over low heat for at least 30 minutes, stirring occasionally.

4. Adjust seasonings to taste.

Rehydrating TVP

Most of the time, TVP needs to be rehydrated in hot water for 8–10 minutes in order to be fully rehydrated, unless it will be hydrated when cooking, such as in a soup with extra liquid. The secret in this recipe is to only partially rehydrate the TVP, so that it absorbs some of the spices from the chili and the liquid from the tomatoes.

Hawaiian Pineapple and Mint Rice Salad

Serves 6

4 cups cooked white rice

2 ribs celery, diced

1 cup diced pineapple (fresh or canned)

⅓ cup chopped macadamia or cashew nuts

¼ cup dried papaya or raisins (optional)

⅓ cup pineapple juice

2 tablespoons olive or safflower oil

2 tablespoons red wine vinegar

¼ cup toasted coconut flakes

2 tablespoons chopped fresh mint

Quickly toasting coconut flakes brings out their nutty bounty of flavor. Place the coconut flakes on an ungreased skillet over low heat, stirring constantly. Toast them just until you see the slightest bit of golden brown on the edges, then remove the pan from the heat.

1. Combine the cooked rice, celery, pineapple, macadamia, and dried papaya together in a large bowl.

2. In a separate small bowl, whisk together the pineapple juice, oil, and vinegar. Toss together with rice and coat well. Chill for at least 1 hour.

3. Gently toss with coconut flakes and mint just before serving.

Index

Note: Page numbers in **bold** indicate recipe category lists.

the hungry
Editor

Foodies Unite!

Bring your appetite and follow The Hungry Editor who really loves to eat. She'll be discussing (and drooling over) all things low-fat and full-fat, local and fresh, canned and frozen, highbrow and lowbrow. . .

When it comes to good eats, The Hungry Editor (and her tastebuds) do not discriminate!

It's a Feeding Frenzy—dig in!

Sign up for our newsletter at

www.adamsmedia.com/blog/cooking

and download our free **Top Ten Gourmet Meals for $7** recipes!